French Cooking For Every Home
La Cuisine Francaise Adapted To American Requirements

by Francois Tanty

Late "Chef de Cuisine" to the Emperor Napoleon III and of the Imperial Russian Family.

with an introduction by Miss Georgia Goodblood
(Introduction Copyright 2017 by Miss. Georgia Goodblood)

This work contains material that was originally published in 1893.

This publication is within the Public Domain.

This edition is reprinted for educational purposes
and in accordance with all applicable Federal Laws.

Self Reliance Books

Get more historic titles on animal and stock breeding, gardening and old fashioned skills by visiting us at:

http://selfreliancebooks.blogspot.com/

INTRODUCTION

It is with much enthusiasm that I present to you the recipes of a truly great French Chef, Francois Tanty, once *Chef de Cuisine* to the Emperor of France, Napoleon III, and to the Imperial Family of Russia.

This is a very old cookery book, first published in 1893, but you will recognize many French classic dishes, and some you may never have tried, nor even heard of. But this great book is a kitchen essential for both novices or professionals alike, as it contains some of the greatest French dishes ever created.

I hope you enjoy this recipe book, and may it aid you in filling your home with the tantalizing aromas of fine French food.

Bon appetit!
Miss. Georgia Goodblood
State of Jefferson, 2017.

INTRODUCTION.

MY dear readers, my intention is not to publish in the following pages an extensive volume, full of long and complicated recipes, but to tell you how, at a small expense, cooking may be made not only substantial and wholesome, but also appetizing and palatable. "The Creator by obliging men to eat to sustain life"—says Brillat Savarin—"invites him by the appetite and rewards him by the pleasure;" but to have real pleasure while at the table, and this pleasure is of every age, it is necessary that the meal presented to you should please at the same time the smell, the taste and the view.

"A ce propos" I cannot protest enough against the custom so general in the United States to give to the table only the necessary time and to eat like a locomotive taking water, by doing which you expose yourself to the various stomach diseases which make so rapidly the fortune of the doctors and druggists

To this my male readers will certainly respond: "We are so busy, we haven't time;" well, let us excuse them for taking the least time possible at lunch; business is business and the lunch not an important meal, but in many cases the one to blame for the hastening of dinner is the housewife who does not give to the dinner all the care it requires.

It is certainly not through lack of good will, because the Americans love home and do their utmost to make it comfortable and attractive, but a good cook is a rare and expensive blessing here and sometimes the mistress of the house does not know anything about cooking.

Why does she not consult one of the numerous books written on the matter? There are certainly many of them; but unfortunately the great majority are intelligible only to professional cooks, because the chief object of the authors has been to gain reputation among their fellow cooks.

My manner of procedure will be entirely different; wishing above all to be clear and practical, therefore I will not hesitate to simplify the recipe of a dish, while keeping its consecrated name; it will be perhaps a little less refined, but quite as palatable and after all will be feasible for all housekeepers, providing they take the trouble of following my advice.

Now let us begin at the beginning, that is to indicate how a " Menu " shall be arranged.

A family dinner is essentially composed of:

A soup.

A fish or meat with sauce and vegetable called " Entree."

A roast, meat, poultry or game.

A vegetable of the season, dried or preserved called "Entremet" (side dish).

A sweet dish, ice cream, or some pastry.

Cheese and fruit.

Providing the dinner becomes more fashionable, you should serve two kinds of soup, a clear one and a puree or cream, from which the guest may choose; and increase the number of entrees and entremets.

A last advice before giving some examples of menus: To give pleasure a dinner should have variety, and consequently you must avoid serving the same dish or sauce twice, palatable as it may be; and as a rule a dish with white sauce should follow a dish with red or brown sauce; for instance in the second family menu given below we could not place "fillets of sole," with shrimp sauce, after the "Andalousian soup," both being red, nor after the "cream of fowl," of the holiday dinner, a fish with " Hollandaise sauce," both being white; that will injure at once the eye and the palate of an epicure.

There are now to start with two quite simple family dinners:

SOUP.

Stock soup—*Clear.*

ENTREE (meat).

Chateaubriand—*Brown.*

Fried Potatoes.

ENTREMET.

Mushrooms on Toast—*White.*

ROAST.

Roast Fowl—*Brown.*

SWEET DISH.

Peach à la Condé—*White.*

SOUP.

Andalousian Soup—*Red.*

ENTREE (fish).

Salmon Trout.

With Hollandaise Sauce —*White.*

Boiled Potatoes.

ROAST.

Leg of Lamb with Mint Sauce—*Brown.*

ENTREMET.

Croquettes of Oatmeal a l'Indienne—*Red.*

SWEET DISH.

Eggs a la Neige—*White.*

The following menu is for a holiday, and by adding one or two entremets it may serve for a banquet :

SOUPS.

Cream of Fowl—*White.*

Printanier—*Clear and brown.*

HORS D'OEUVRES.

Radishes, Olives and Anchovies.

ENTREES.

Fillets of Trout with Shrimp sauce—*Red.* Boiled potatoes.

Saddle of Mutton Richelieu—*Brown.*

ENTREMET.

Celery a la Moelle—*White.*

ROAST.

Roast Snipe on Toast—*Brown.*

Salad.

SWEET DISHES.

Pudding Diplomate—*Yellow.*

Pistachio Ice Cream with Cakes—*Green.*

FRUITS.

HOW TO SET A TABLE.

AT first glance nothing pleases the eye of a guest more than a well set table, that is to say, where elegance is combined with good taste. On that matter Americans need very little advice, because, as a rule, they are very fond of fine linen and decorations of fruit and flowers.

Therefore, we will give only practical hints, taking as example a dinner quite fashionable, leaving to the housewife the care of simplifying the same for family dinners.

The table should be spacious enough to avoid the crowding of dishes or covers, and to permit the guests being comfortably seated.

There are many ways of decorating a table, the following being the one our experience has proven to be the best:

Place a center piece of flowers, around which (and according to the size of the table) may be disposed smaller pieces of flowers, fruits, bon-bons, etc., and also the "Hors d'Oeuvres" served in special small dishes.

Candle light being more fashionable than gas, and also more beautifying for the ladies, candelabra should be placed in sufficient number.

Before each plate place the necessary number of glasses, of different sizes, according to the wines that are to be served; this number not to surpass five, viz:

A glass for water.
A glass for white wine, claret and burgundy.
A glass for madeira, sherry and sweet dessert wines.
A glass for Rhine wine (if served).*
A glass or cup for champagne.

Don't fill the water glass before the dinner, but place decanters and crystal bowls filled with pieces of ice, within the easy reach of the guests.

At the *right* of each cover the knife, fork and spoon (the former having a *sharp steel* blade). These should be changed with each course.

Before the cover a set of smaller knife, fork and spoon for the sweet dishes and dessert. This last knife should have a silver blade.

---

*This glass is usually green or amber.

The napkin should be of good size, placed on the *plate*, folded, with a small roll between the folds.

Between each cover should be a salt cellar; for the pepper the best is to have some pepper mills with *white* whole pepper.

Before each cover, and supported by the glass should be a "Menu" (bill of fare) printed or hand-written; it will prove more convenient if on each card you write the name of the particular guest who will occupy the place.

The meats should be carved in the kitchen, but the parts put together in a way to represent the whole piece; they will be distributed by the host or the hostess, or, better, the dish shall be presented at the *left* of every guest (the ladies first) so that each may serve himself, with the right hand, according to his taste.

In every dinner "á la Française" wine is served; the number, kinds and quality varying of course according to the importance of the dinner.

This is the general order in which they are served, viz:

After the soup.—A strong dry wine such as madeira, or sherry.

With the fish.—A white dry wine such as Sauternes, Chablis, Chateau d'Yquem, Rhine wine, etc.

After the fish and until the roast.—Claret.

With the roast.—Burgundy.

With sweet dishes.—Champagnes or dessert wines such as Tokay, Malaga, Constance, etc.

As a last advice, remember the old adage: "The dinner should never await the guests, but the guests the dinner, because, however well cooked, a dish cannot be warmed over."

PUBLISHERS' NOTES.

•••••••••••••••

IN the translating and collaborating of this excellent work we are
indebted to M. Louis Tanty, who attended to the systematic
arrangement which tends to so greatly simplify the book that
no one can complain of its difficulties, even with the most
elaborate dishes.

M. François Tanty, the author, was trained for his profession under
Carême, the most noted cook of his day; M. Tanty then became chef of
Emperor Napoleon III. of France, leaving this office for that of chef of
the imperial family of Russia, where he attained a rank similar to that
of Colonel in the Russian army, and was decorated by the late Czar with
the Imperial Order of the Red Cross (see back cover page), in considera-
tion of his services as purveyor to the Army and Hospital Corps in the
Russian-Turkish war. M. Tanty was also proprietor of the Grand Hotel
and the famous restaurant Dussaux at St. Petersburg, the latter probably
the finest in the world. About three years ago he came to America to
establish his sons in business, and thus has been able to adapt the re-
quirements of his wonderful cuisine to the American home.

French cooking is proverbial for its elegance, simplicity and cheap-
ness, so this book will prove a genuine economic blessing to the housewife, while developing her culinary skill.

THE SOUPS.

In this chapter we will describe the principal soups which can be made easily by any housewife. By modifying some of the recipes: for instance, by replacing in a puree one kind of vegetable for another, by game instead of fowl, or by varying the garnishing, she will have quite an infinite number of soups at her disposal. She should be careful, however, always to follow the general rules given and not to forget that anything printed in italics is always something essential.

The soup beginning the dinner should be at the same time palatable and light, to prepare but not to overload the stomach.

The soups are divided into two classes: the clear ones, whose nature is well indicated by the name, and the mixed or thick ones, that is to say, those into which, as into the puree and cream, enter eggs, flour or starch. Both of these two classes may contain either lean or fat soups.

1. BOUILLON.

STOCK SOUP. (*Fat Soup—Clear.*)

Stock being the foundation of fat soups, and serving also to prepare numerous sauces and dishes, it would prove advantageous for a housekeeper to always have some stock at her disposal. This is quite easy, as stock may be kept fresh for several days in an ice box, preferably in an earthen jar, the only precaution necessary being to let it boil awhile, in case of a very hot or stormy day, to prevent its turning sour.

To obtain a very good stock use at the same time beef, veal and fowl, the proportions being 6 parts of beef, 2 of veal, and 1 of fowl.

As the beef gives the greatest part of the strength and nutriment, it may be used alone, but it will be at the expense of the aroma and delicacy of the stock.

Moreover, the veal to be used being the shin bone, which is worth a mere nothing, and the fowl old hens, the expense will be scarcely increased.

BEEF.—The parts of the beef to be employed for stock are: the neck, shoulder, shin, ribs, flank, round, legs; add also some marrow bones if you omit the veal.

Don't forget that the meat must be very fresh, otherwise the bouillon will be inferior in every respect.

VEAL.—The part to be employed is the *shin bone* or *hock*, which is very rich in gelatinous principles.

FOWL.—Employ old fowls rather than young chickens, the former giving more taste, and having to be boiled quite a long time, it matters not if they are old and tough.

VEGETABLES. — They should be very fresh and pared only when wanted for use.

SALT.—Don't put in too much salt, because in some of its uses the bouillon may be associated with some preparations already salted and this will prove disagreeable.

PROPORTIONS.—1. For a family of five and only for one meal:

```
Beef and bones...........5 lbs.
Veal.....................½ hock (about 2 lbs.).
Fowl ....................The body of 1 hen.
Vegetables...............2 carrots, ¼ turnip, 1 onion, some celery.
Water....................From 3 to 4 quarts.
```
Time.—About 5 hours.

2. To prepare 3 gallons of bouillon to be kept for culinary purposes:

```
Beef...............15 lbs.
Veal...............1 hock (about 5 lbs.).
Fowl*..............1 hen, or the bodies of 2.
Vegetables......4 carrots, 1 turnip, 1 leek, some celery, 2 onions.
Water...........3½ gallons (about).
```
Time.—About 5 hours.

REMARKS.—One of the onions should be halved and browned on the stove before being put in the soup to give color and taste. When only one onion is used you brown one of the halves. You may also put one or two cloves in the part of the onion which has not been browned.

PREPARATION.—1st. Let the cold water from the faucet run freely over your beef and veal so as to wash them from all impurities. Put

* Boiled chicken served with a white sauce and rice is a very good family dish; the flesh of the chickens serve also for chicken croquettes,

them in a kettle with the necessary quantity of water,* cold water and not hot or warm, taking care that the water covers the meat well but does not reach higher than two inches from the edge of the kettle. 2d. Allow to boil slowly while scumming until clear. It will prove advantageous to add from time to time one spoonful of cold water, which will facilitate and accelerate the separation of the scum. 3d. When the stock is clear (after half an hour) add your vegetables which should have been pared only a little while before, to be fresh, and let boil for two (2) hours. 4th. Take the veal out of the pot, as all juices will have been extracted from it, add the fowl and let the soup boil slowly for another three (3) hours.† 5th. Take the floating grease off, and pass through a strainer or napkin.

CLARIFICATION.—If it happens that your stock is not clear, having perhaps boiled too quickly, you may clarify it as follows: 1st. Put your kettle on the corner of the range so that, though very hot, it doesn't boil. 2d. Break into a bowl or sauce pan 2 eggs with their shells, beat with ½ or 1 pound chopped meat, and 1 or 2 glassesful of water. Add while beating from 3 to 5 glasses of stock and pour the whole in the kettle while stirring. 4th. Pass the stock through a strainer and then through a napkin.

2. CONSOMME.

(*Fat Soup—Clear.*)

We call *consomme* a stock stronger and more palatable than the common one. It forms the fundament of the soups for fashionable dinners, or is served in cups at a ball supper or a select lunch. It is also very convenient for sick or feeble persons.

PROPORTIONS.—For five persons:

Fowl...................1.
Veal hock..........½.
Vegetables.. ....1 carrot, 1 onion, some celery.
Stock...................3 to 4 quarts.
Time.—About 2½ hours.

PREPARATION.—1st. Cut to pieces the fowl and the veal, let them cook in some butter until a light brown; then put them in a kettle with the necessary amount of stock. 2d. Allow to cook slowly for two hours while scumming from time to time. 3d. Take the floating grease off and pass through a napkin.

---

* Hot water would obstruct the pores of the meat thus enclosing juices as well as impurities.

† Place your kettle on the corner of the range so that ebullition takes place only on one side of the kettle. In this way it is easier to obtain a clear soup.

3. CONSOMME DE VOLAILLE.

CONSOMME OF FOWL. (*Fat Soup—Clear.*)

Do as above (No. 2) but before serving take the fillets of the fowl off, cut them in dices and serve the consomme with those dices of flesh and 1½ tablespoonsful of rice previously cooked apart in some salted water and carefully dripped.

4. POT AU FEU.

(*Fat Soup—Clear.*)

PROPORTIONS.—For five persons:
  Stock...................2 to 3 quarts.
  Vegetables...........2 carrots, 1 onion, ½ head of cabbage, 1 leek, some celery.
  Time.—1¾ to 2 hours.

PREPARATION.—1st. Slice your vegetables quite fine, let them cook in some boiling water until quite soft and let them drip through a strainer. Put the vegetables in an empty sauce pan or kettle, pour over the necessary quantity of stock and allow to cook slowly for 1½ hours.

5. CROUTE AU POT.

(*Fat Soup—Clear.*)

The *Croute au Pot* is a *Pot au Feu* served with some pieces of toast in the soup.

6. PRINTANIER.

(*Fat Soup—Clear.*) Two hours.

NOTE.—The denomination "Printanier" comes from "Printemps," spring, and in this soup may enter all the vegetables produced by the spring, viz: young turnips, carrots, cauliflowers, Brussels sprouts, etc., points of asparagus and hops, green peas and beans, etc.

The carrots and turnips must be as tender as possible, and you cut them in small dices or better in small balls or ovals with a vegetable spoon; the Brussels sprouts and the cauliflower shall not exceed the size of a hazel nut; the green peas shall be chosen as fine as possible and the green beans cut in small lozenges.

PROPORTIONS.—For five persons:
  Stock or consomme.........2 or 3 quarts.
  Vegetables ....About 3 tablespoonsful.

PREPARATION.—Do as for "pot au feu;" for fine dinners use consomme instead of stock.

7. BRUNOISE.

(*Fat Soup—Clear.*) Two hours.

The brunoise is a simplified printanier, only carrots, turnips and green peas being used, the two former cut in small dices.

8. JULIENNE.

(*Fat Soup—Clear.*)

PROPORTIONS.—For five persons:

Stock or consomme...2 to 3 quarts.
Vegetables............1 carrot, ⅛ turnip, ₁₀ cabbage, ⅛ leek. (All very fresh.)
Time.—About 1¾ hours.

PREPARATION.—1st. Slice your vegetables into "julienne," that is to say into fine strips about 1½ inches long, put them in a sauce pan with some butter and a teaspoonful of sugar; let cook awhile. 2d. Pour your stock or consomme over and allow to cook for 1½ hours.*

9. POTAGE COLBERT.

SOUP A LA COLBERT. (*Fat Soup—Clear*).

PROPORTIONS.—For five persons:

Printanier or brunoise...2 to 3 quarts.
Poached eggs...5.

PREPARATION.—Make a printanier or brunoise as above, but with little vegetables and when in the tureen add a poached egg for each person.

NOTE.—There are different methods to poach eggs, but the following is the easiest and best. 1st. Pour your eggs in as much boiling water as will not stop the ebullition and let them boil for six minutes. 2d. Take the eggs out with a skimmer and pour cold water over them. (This will facilitate the shelling of the eggs.) 3d. Take the shells off carefully and put the eggs in the soup only when ready to serve.

10. CONSOMME AU RIZ.

CONSOMME WITH RICE. (*Fat Soup—Clear.*)

PROPORTIONS.—For five persons:

Stock or consomme...2 to 3 quarts.
Rice...⅛ tablespoonful.

PREPARATION.—1st. Wash your rice and let it boil in some water till soft. 2d. Let it drip, *cool it with cold water* and let it drip again.

---

* What distinguishes the "Julienne" from the former soups is that in this one the vegetables are not previously cooked in boiling water.

3d. Warm your stock or consomme and when ready to serve put the rice in the soup which you must not allow to boil again.

11. CONSOMME AU VERMICELLE.

VERMICELLI. (*Fat Soup—Clear.*)

12. CONSOMME AU MACARONI.

MACARONI. (*Fat Soup—Clear.*)

PROPORTIONS.—

Stock or consomme...2 to 8 quarts.
Vermicelli or macaroni ....2 ounces.

PREPARATION.—1st. Break your vermicelli in pieces 1 inch long or the macaroni in pieces ⅓ inch long and let either cook in some boiling water and do as indicated above for the rice.   (2d and 3d.)

13. POTAGE MILANAISE.

PROPORTIONS.—

Stock or consomme...2 to 3 quarts.
Macaroni..¼ lb.
Rasped cheese (Parmesan preferred).....................2 oz.

PREPARATION.—As for the above, but when ready to serve add the rasped cheese and some white pepper.

14. POTAGE "OXTAIL."

OXTAIL SOUP.   (*Fat Soup—Half thick.*)

PROPORTIONS.—For five persons:

Oxtail...1.
Vegetables..1 carrot, 1 onion.
Madeira...1 glassful.
Corn starch...1 small tablespoonful.
Red pepper..A little.
Stock...2 to 3 quarts.

PREPARATION.—1st. Take one oxtail, cut it in pieces one inch long let it boil in some water until tender.   2d. Let it drip, pare it to take off the grease and small bones.   3d. Put it in a sauce pan with 2 or 3 quarts of bouillon, ⅓ glass madeira, 1 onion and 1 carrot, some thyme and laurel.   Let the whole cook for 3 hours.   4th. Pour the bouillon through a strainer in another sauce pan, take off the floating grease, add ⅓ of a glass of madeira, a little red pepper; allow to cook awhile and when ready to serve add, while stirring, 1 tablespoonful of corn starch mixed with 1 glass *cold* bouillon.   5th. Serve in a tureen in which you place the pieces of the tail.

15. POTAGE TORTUE.

TURTLE SOUP. (*Fat Soup—Half thick.*)

The real name should be "Mock Turtle," but prepared as follows this soup may replace the "genuine" turtle soup with advantage.

PROPORTIONS.—For five persons:

Calf Head............½.
Vegetables...........2 onions, 3 carrots, some celery, thyme and laurel.
Mushrooms, truffles, cockscombs, "ad libitum."
Maderia ....1 glassful.
Vinegar...............½ glassful.
Flour..................2 tablespoonsful.
Starch................1 tablespoonful.
Caramel ....⎫
Red pepper.......⎬ A little.
Whole pepper...⎭
Stock...................2 or 3 quarts.

PREPARATION.—Have the ½ of a calf's head, take the bone off, put the meat in a kettle with cold water; allow it to boil while skimming carefully for about ten minutes. 2d. Put the meat in cold water to cool it, let it drip. 3d. Put the meat in another kettle with two tablespoonsful of flour and add ¼ gallon cold water, while stirring, and one-half (½) glass vinegar (this for the purpose of keeping the calf white), add 2 onions, 3 carrots, some thyme and laurel, some whole pepper, let boil one hour and skim. 4th. Allow the meat to drip, press the same between two loaded plates until cold. 5th. Cut the cold calf's head in dices, put them in a pan with mushrooms (also truffles, cockscombs), 1 glassful madeira, 2 quarts stock, let boil awhile and skim. 6th. When ready to serve add a little *caramel** (to give color), a little cayenne pepper and a cup of bouillon in which you have mixed 1 tablespoonful of corn starch.

* We call burned sugar caramel.

16. MULLAGATAWNEY.

(Fat Soup—Half thick.)

PROPORTIONS.—For five persons :

Fowl.........................1 young chicken or the giblets of some.
Ham (lean)..................4 ounces.
Butter.........................1 tablespoonful.
Vegetables...................1 carrot, 1 onion, 1 celery.
Flour...........................1½ tablespoonful.
Red pepper............... } A little.
Sugar....................... }
Stock..........................2 to 3 quarts.

Time—1 hour.

PREPARATION. — 1st.   Chop yonr onion fine and let it cook in a sauce pan to a light brown, add then the chicken cut in pieces about 2 inches long, the ham, carrots and celery cut in dices.   2d.   Allow the whole to cook a while, sift the flour in while stirring, add 2 to 3 quarts of stock.   3d.   Let cook slowly for ½ hour longer if the chicken is not tender.   4th.   Take the floating grease off, add a little bit of pepper and sugar and put in the tureen 1½ tablespoonsful rice (cooked as indicated in 10).

17. TCHY A LA RUSSE.

RUSSIAN TCHY.   *(Fat—Half thick.)*

PROPORTIONS.—For five persons:

Beef breast..........................6 lbs.
Vegetables............................½ cabbage, 2 carrots, 2 onions.
Water.....................................2 to 3 quarts.
Flour.....................................2 tablespoonsful.
Sour cream ....1 glassful.

PREPARATION.—1st. Take 6 lbs. of beef breast, cut it into pieces about 1 inch long, place it in a kettle with two to three quarts *cold* water, let boil while skimming.   2d. When the bouillon begins to be clear, add ½ cabbage, 2 carrots, 2 onions, sliced quite fine, and let cook for about 3 hours.   3d. When quite ready to serve, mix in a bowl 2 tablespoonsful of flour with about 1 glass bouillon (not too warm), pour in the kettle while stirring, add 1 glass of sour cream and serve hot; the soup and meat being served together in the tureen.

NOTE.—In winter time the Russians replace the fresh cabbage with sour krout.

18. POTAGE SEMOULE LIEE.

SEMOLIA SOUP.   *(Fat Soup.—Half thick.)*

PROPORTIONS.—For five persons:

Semolia................¼ lb.	Yolks......................2.
Cream...................1 glassful.	Stock.................2 to 3 quarts.

Time.—¾ hour.

PREPARATION.—1st. Warm the stock in a sauce pan till it boils, then sift the semolia in and pour slowly with the left hand while stirring with the right one, so as to mix well. 2d. Allow to cook for ⅓ hour and when ready to serve, pour in the sauce pan (which has been set on a corner of the range) 1 glassful of cream mixed with the two yolks, stirring all the time.

19. POTAGE A L'ORGE.

BARLEY SOUP. (*Fat Soup—Half thick.*)

PROPORTIONS.—For five persons:

Barley. ....3 tablespoonsful.	Butter ....1 tablespoonful.
Yolk ....1.	Stock ....2 to 3 quarts.
Cream...........1 glassful.	*Time.*—2¾ hours.

PREPARATION.—1st. Wash your barley and let it stand for ⅓ hour in some cold water. 2d. Let it drip and let it cook till soft in some boiling water. 3d. Let it drip, cool with some cold water and let it drip again. 4th. Put your barley with your stock in a sauce pan and allow to cook for one hour. 5th. When ready to serve, beat in a bowl 1 yolk, 1 glassful cream, 1 tablespoonful butter; add little by little while stirring some of the soup, then, placing the sauce pan on a corner of the range, pour the mixture in while stirring, but do not let the soup boil again.

20. POTAGE ANDALOUX.

TOMATO SOUP. (*Lean or Fat—Half thick.*)

PROPORTIONS.—For five persons:

Tomatoes..... .⅓ lb.	Corn starch.........1 teaspoonful.
Vegetables....1 carrot, 1 onion,	Butter..................1 tablespoonful.
some thyme and laurel.	Stock or water.....2 quarts.
Rice............1¼ tablespoonful.	*Time.*—1¼ hours.

PREPARATION.—1st. Put in a sauce pan ⅓ lb. can of tomatoes (or ⅓ lb. fresh tomatoes which you have scalded apart in some boiling water) with 1 carrot and 1 onion minced, some thyme and laurel, let cook 1 hour. 2d. Sift the whole through a strainer, add 2 quarts stock or water, salt, white pepper and cayenne pepper. 3d. Pour in 1 teaspoonful of corn starch mixed in a little cold water and one tablespoon of good butter. 4th. When ready to serve add 1¼ tablespoonsful of rice cooked apart. (No. 10.)

21. BORCH A LA POLONAISE.

BEET SOUP. (*Fat—Half thick.*)

Red beets.........3	Stock or water......2 to 3 quarts.
Vegetables ......1 onion, ⅛	Flour..................⅛ tablespoonful.
head cabbage.	Milk....................1 glassful.
Butter ....1 tablespoonful.	*Time.*—1¼ hours.

PREPARATION.—1st. Clean and mince 2 red beets, 1 onion, ⅛ of a cabbage, put the whole in a sauce pan with some butter, cook awhile, then add ⅓ tablespoonful of flour and 2 to 3 quarts of stock, cook 1 hour. 2d. Grate 1 red beet, press it through a napkin and when ready to serve pour the juice in the soup and add a glassful of milk.

22. POTAGE A LA REINE.

CREAM OF FOWL. (*Fat—Half thick.*)

PROPORTIONS.—For five persons:

Fowl........................... 1 hen or chicken.
Vegetables.................. 1 onion, 1 carrot, 1 stalk of celery.
Water........................ 2 to 3 quarts.

Time—2½ hours.

PREPARATION. - 1st. Take one chicken and allow it to cook for 2 hours in ½ gallon of water with ½ veal or beef knuckle, 1 onion, 1 carrot, 1 sprig of celery. 2d. When the chicken is quite tendor let it drip and strain the stock through a napkin. 3d. Take the chicken off, put the fillets apart and pound the remainder of the flesh in a mortar. 4th. Add, little by little, while beating, the stock, and sift that paste through a sifter so as to obtain a pap. 5th. Let melt in a sauce pan 2 tablespoonsful of butter with 1½ tablespoonsful of flour; pour the pap in, let it become hot, but don't allow it to boil. When ready to serve add the chicken fillets, cut into small dices.

23. CREME DE CELERI.

CREAM OF CELERY. (*Fat—Half thick.*)

PROPORTIONS.—For five persons:

Celery.........5 stalks.	Yolks ....3.
Flour..........3 tablespoonsful.	Sugar...............½ teaspoonful.
Butter.........3 tablespoonsful.	Cream ....1 glassful.
Stock..........2 to 3 quarts.	

PREPARATION.—1st. Wash and clean the celery stalks, let them boil in water for 5 minutes, let them drip, cool them with cold water and let them drip again. 2d. Chop the celery stalks, put them in a sauce pan with 2 tablespoonsful butter and 3 tablespoonsful flour, allow the whole to cook awhile and add the stock. 3d. Let cook altogether for 1 hour, pass through a sifter, and put the pap in a sauce pan and heat it hot. 4th. When ready to serve make a "liaison" with 3 yolks, 1 glass cream, 2 tablespoonsful butter, and do as indicated above in No. 22. (See page 27, General Remarks.)

24. CREME D'ASPERGES.

CREAM OF ASPARAGUS. (*Fat—Half thick.*)

As for the above, but use three bunches of asparagus instead of celery.

25. CREME DE CHOUX FLEURS.

CREAM OF CAULIFLOWER. (*Fat—Half thick.*)

As for the above, except use the white part of one cauliflower.

26. PUREE CRECY.

CARROT SOUP. (*Fat or Lean—Half thick.*)

PROPORTIONS.—For five persons:

Carrot....................6.	Flour..............1 tablespoonful,
Onion....................1.	Rice ....1½ tablespoonsful.
Butter...................1 tablespoonful.	Stock or water..2 to 3 quarts.

PREPARATION.—1st. Cut your carrots in small dices, and let them cook in a sauce pan with some butter and a chopped onion. 2d. Add while stirring, 1 tablespoonful of flour and 2 to 3 quarts stock or water and let cook slowly for 1 hour. 3d. Pass through a sifter or strainer, and when ready to serve add 1 tablespoonful good butter and 1½ table-spoonsful rice cooked separately. (No. 10.)

27. POTAGE ST. GERMAIN.

GREEN PEA SOUP. (*Fat or Lean—Half thick.*)

PROPORTIONS AND PREPARATION.—Same as for the foregoing No. 26, but take fresh (or dried) green peas instead of beans. Serve with fried dices of bread sprinkled over.

28. POTAGE CONDE.

WHITE KIDNEY BEAN SOUP. (*Fat or Lean—Half thick.*)

PROPORTIONS.—For five persons:

White kidney beans......... ...1 pint	Butter ....2 tablespoonsful.
Onions................................2.	Stock or water...2 to 3 quarts.

PREPARATION.—Take 1 pint white kidney beans, let them cook in some salted water with one sliced onion. 2d. When well cooked sift through a strainer or a sifter, put this pap in a sauce pan with 2 to 3 quarts stock or water, and when ready to serve add 2 tablespoonsful of butter. Serve hot with small toasts apart.

29. POTAGE MUSARD.

RED KIDNEY BEAN SOUP. (*Fat or Lean—Half thick.*)

PROPORTIONS AND PREPARATION.—As for the above, but replace *white* kidney beans by red ones.

30. CREME DE LENTILLES.

LENTIL SOUP. (*Fat or Lean--Half thick.*)

PROPORTIONS AND PREPARATION.—Same as above, but use lentils.

31. POTAGE PAYSANNE.

VEGETABLE SOUP. (*Lean—Clear.*)

PROPORTIONS.—For five persons:
Vegetables.............Cabbage ⅛, carrot 1, potato 1, turnip ⅓,
                    onion ⅓, some celery.
Water..................2 to 3 quarts.
Milk......................1 glassful.
Butter ....1 tablespoonful.
Time —1½ hours.

PREPARATION.—1st. Take ⅛ cabbage, 1 carrot, 1 potato, ⅓ turnip, ⅓ onion, some celery, mince them all, then wash and let drip. 2d. Put those minced vegetables in a sauce pan with 2 to 3 quarts of water and a little salt, allow them to boil for 1½ hours. When ready to serve add 1 glass milk, 1 tablespoonful butter and some pieces of toast.

32. SOUPE A L'ONION.

ONION SOUP. (*Lean—Clear.*)

PROPORTIONS.—For five persons:
Onions............. ....12 (somewhat according to the size).
Butter...... ....2 tablespoonsful.
Flour..........................1 tablespoonful
Bread..........................⅛ lb.
Rasped cheese...................⅛ lb.
Water..........................2 to 3 quarts.
Time.—1 hour.

PREPARATION.—1st. Have about 12 fine slices of bread and ⅛ lb. of rasped cheese, Parmesan preferred, place some slices on the bottom of a dish that can be put in an oven, pour over a bed of cheese, then a bed of bread, etc., finishing by a bed of bread but preserving enough cheese for a last bed. 2d. Chop about 12 onions, let them cook slowly in a sauce pan with about 2 tablespoonsful of butter until a light brown, add while stirring 1 tablespoonful of flour, stir the whole for a while, then add 2 quarts of water. 3d. Allow to cook for 5 minutes. 4th. Pour this soup through a strainer on the bed prepared as above. 5th. Pour over the dish a last bed of cheese, and let it bake until a light brown.

CAUTION.—In serving this soup take care to give each guest some of the crust, dry and palatable.

NOTE.—You may have a good family soup by doing only as indicated in the 2d. and 3d. and serving it with some toast and rasped cheese.

33. SOUPE A L'OSEILLE.

SORREL SOUP. (*Lean—Half Clear.*)

PROPORTIONS.—

Sorrel	1 lb.	Cream	1 glassful.
Butter	3 tablespoonsful.	Water	2 or 3 quarts.
Flour	1 tablespoonful.	Bread for toast	Ad libitum.
Eggs	2.	*Time.*—⅓ hour.	

PREPARATION.—1st. Clean, wash and let drip 1 lb. sorrel. 2d. Chop it fine and let it cook slowly for 5 minutes in a sauce pan with two table-spoonsful of butter. 3d. Add while stirring 1 tablespoonful of flour and and 2 or 3 quarts water. Let boil awhile. 4th. Beat in a bowl 1 glassful of cream, 2 eggs, 1 tablespoonful butter; take the saucepan on a corner of the range and pour the contents of the bowl in while stirring. Don't allow to boil again and serve with some slices of bread or toast.

34. OUKA DE PERCHES A LA MOSCOVITE.

RUSSIAN FISH SOUP. (*Lean—Clear.*)

PROPORTIONS.—For five persons:

Fresh perch	4 lbs.
Vegetables	2 onions, 4 carrots, 4 stalks of celery, some parsley, thyme and laurel.
	Time.—1 hour.

PREPARATION.—1st. Clean and wash carefully about 4 lbs. very fresh perch. Take the fillets off and put them apart. 2d. Put the heads and the back bones in a kettle with two onions, 2 carrots, 2 celery stalks, some parsley, thyme and laurel, 2 quarts of water, a little salt, let boil for 1 hour. 3d. Slice in "julienne" (See No. 8.), 2 celery stalks and 2 carrots. let them cook in some water until quite tender, then let them drip. 4th. Put the dripped vegetables in a sauce pan with the fillets, pour over the fish "stock" and let cook again for ¼ hour.

This soup, which may be made with quite every kind of fish, pro-vided it is very fresh, can be served advantageously with lean dinners and is matchless for camping parties.

35. BOUILLABAISSE.

(*Lean—Clear.*)

NOTE.—If this recipe is not the one of the "genuine" Bouillabaise of Marseille, it will enable our reader to obtain a delicious soup, perhaps more palatable than the genuine. I composed this recipe especially for the late Emperor of Russia, who was very fond of fish soup, but did not like to find "fish bones" in his plate.

PROPORTIONS.—For five persons:

Redsnapper............1.		Thyme and laurel....Some.	
Dorade or pike.......1.		Soffran..................A little.	
Perch...................2.		Butter ....1 tablespoonful.	
Lobster (alive)........1.		Bread.....................½ lb.	
Vegetables............1 onion, 6 toma-		White wine............1 pint.	
toes, 2 cloves of garlic.		Water ....2 to 3 quarts.	

PREPARATION.—1st. Clean and wash your fishes, take the fillets off and put them aside on a dish; cut off the small paws and the extremity of the lobster's tail, put them apart in a mortar to be broken fine, cut the claws in two, then turn the lobster (placing its back on the table) and cut the tail in slices ½ inch thick and the body in 4 parts, lengthwise and then across. (Always turn a lobster when you wish to divide it.) Place these pieces of lobster apart with your fillets. 2d. Put two chopped onions in a sauce pan with some butter, or olive oil, let cook until a light brown, add the heads and the bones of the fishes, the paws of the lobster broken fine, 1 pint white wine, 2 quarts water, 6 sliced tomatoes, 2 crushed cloves of garlic, some thyme and laurel, some soffran (Spanish soffran); let cook from ⅓ to ¾ hour. 3d. 20 minutes before serving dispose your fillets and pieces of lobster in a hollow dish, pour the fish "stock" over through a *fine strainer*, let boil while scumming for about 10 minutes and serve with some toasts apart.

36. SOUPE AUX HUITRES.

OYSTER SOUP. (*Lean—Clear.*)

PROPORTIONS.—For five persons:

Oysters...................5 dozen.		Cream..................½ glassful.	
White wine............1 glassful.		Butter..................2 tablespoonsful.	
Yolks ....3.		Water or stock ......1 quart.	

Time.—⅓ hour.

PREPARATION.—1st. Take your oysters from the shell, put them with their juice and 1 glassful white wine in a sauce pan, let cook awhile until firm. 2d. Let the oysters drip, pour the juice in a sauce pan through a strainer, and place the oysters on a folded napkin to dry them well. 3d. Add in the sauce pan 1 quart of water or stock, let boil awhile and scum. 4th. When ready to serve beat in a bowl 3 yolks, ½ glassful of cream, 3 tablespoonsful of butter, add in the sauce pan while stirring (as indicated page 27, General Remarks) and pour in a tureen where you have placed the oysters in advance.

37. SOUPE AUX CLAMS.

CLAM SOUP. (*Lean—Clear.*)

PROPORTIONS.—For five persons:

Clams ....2 dozen.
Vegetables.............................1 onion, 1 carrot, 1 parsley root.
Butter ....2 tablespoonsful.
Lemon.....................................1.

Time.—1 hour.

PREPARATION.—1st. Cut in dices 1 onion, 1 carrot, 1 parsley root, let cook the whole for five minutes in some butter; add then water and allow to cook again slowly for ¾ hour. 2d. Take 2 dozen clams off their shells, put them with their juice in a bowl, and when ready to serve pour the whole in a sauce pan, allow to boil for 5 minutes, add 1 tablespoonful of good butter mixed with some hashed parsley. Serve with sliced lemons.

38. POTAGE VELOURS.

VELVET SOUP. (*Lean or Fat—Clear.*)

PROPORTIONS.—For five persons:

Corn starch..........3 teaspoonsful. Milk ....1 glassful.
Eggs ....2. Water, milk or stock.2 to 3 quarts.
Butter.................2 tablespoonsful.

Time—½ hour.

PREPARATION.—1st. Let boil your water, milk or stock, and add 3 tablespoonsful corn starch mixed with a glass of cold water, milk or stock. 2d. Let boil for five minutes then add (as indicated page 27, General Remarks) 2 whole eggs, beaten in a bowl with 1 glass milk and 2 tablespoonsful butter.

39. POTAGE PARMENTIER.

POTATO SOUP. (*Lean or Fat—Half Clear.*)

PROPORTIONS.—For five persons:

Vegetables....½ onion, 2 potatoes. Butter.................1 tablespoonful.
Cream...........1 glassful. Water or stock......2 to 3 quarts.

PREPARATION.—1st. Put in a sauce pan ½ minced onion, fry it until it becomes light brown. 2d. Add 2 minced potatoes and fry them for a little while. 3d. Add 2 quarts of bouillon or water; allow it to boil for twenty minutes. 4th. Sift the whole through a sieve and put the puree back in the sauce pan. 5th. When ready to serve add 1 glass cream, mixed with 1 tablespoonful butter without allowing the soup to boil again.

40. POTAGE SEMOULE AU LAIT.

SEMOLIA WITH MILK. (*Lean—Half Thick.*)

PROPORTIONS.—For five persons:

Semolia	¼ lb.	Yolks	2.
Milk	2 to 3 quarts.	Time—	¾ hour.

Do as for No. 18, but mix your yolks with some cold milk.

41. POTAGE PRINCESSE. (Vulgo Panada.)

BREAD SOUP. (*Lean—Thick.*)

PROPORTIONS.—For five persons:

Bread	½ lb.	Cream	1 glass
Eggs	3.	Water	2 quarts.
Butter	3 tablespoonsful.	Time—	1 hour.

PREPARATION.—Let the water boil and when boiling add the bread broken into small pieces. 2d. Allow to cook for ¾ hour while stirring from time to time. 3d. When ready to serve beat in a bowl 3 eggs, 3 tablespoonsful butter and 1 glassful of milk or cream, and do as indicated above. (23, 4th part).

42. CREME DE POTURONS.

CREAM OF PUMPKINS. (*Lean—Half Thick.*)

PROPORTIONS.—For five persons:

Pumpkin	3 to 4 lbs.	Sugar	1 teaspoonful.
Butter	4 tablespoonsful.	Milk	2 to 3 quarts.

PREPARATION.—1st. Take the flesh off and cut it in dices 1 in. square. Let boil in some water till tender. 2d. Sift it through a strainer and put the pap in a sauce pan with 4 tablespoonsful of butter, 1 teaspoonful sugar, a little salt; let boil a while, then add 2 quarts boiling milk, stir well the whole and serve with some fried toast (fried at the time of serving preferred).

43. CREME DE MAIS.

CREAM OF SWEET CORN. (*Lean—Half Thick.*)

PROPORTIONS.—For five persons:

Sweet corn	3 to 4 tablespoonsful.	Cream	1 glassful.
Yolks	2.	Milk	2 quarts.
Butter	2 tablespoonsful.	Time.—	¾ hour.

PREPARATION.—1st. Put the sweet corn in two quarts boiling milk, and let cook while stirring for ¼ hour. 2d. Sift through a sifter, put the pap in a sauce pan and when ready to serve pour in a "liaison" composed of 2 yolks, 1 glassful of cream and 2 tablespoonsful of butter, doing as indicated page 27, General Remarks.

44. CREME DUCHESSE BUCKINGHAM.

CREAM OF ALMONDS. (*Lean—Half Thick.*)

PROPORTIONS.—For five persons:

Sweet almonds......2 lbs.	Sugar...................1 teaspoonful.
Bitter almonds......6 to 8.	Starch.................2 teaspoonsful.
Butter.................2 tablespoonsful.	Milk...................2 quarts.

Time.—1 hour.

PREPARATION.—1st. Skin the almonds (dip in boiling water until the skin is tender, let drip, cool in cold water and let drip again, then take the skin off), put them all except 12 in a mortar with 1 glass milk, break them fine, then add little by little and while mixing with the pestle, about 1 quart of milk. 2d. Put the pap in a napkin and press by turning ends in opposite directions. (This shall be done by 2 persons.) 3d. Put the juice of the almonds in a sauce pan, add another quart of milk, let warm but not boil. 4th. When ready to serve add a "liaison" composed of 2 teaspoonsful corn starch, 1 teaspoonful sugar, some salt, 2 tablespoonsful butter mixed with 1 glassful cold milk and do as above. 5th. Cut the almonds you have preserved in strips, and put them in the tureen and pour the cream over.

45. BISQUE DE HOMARDS.

LOBSTER CREAM. (*Fat Soup—Half Thick.*)

PROPORTIONS.—For five persons:

Lobsters.........2 cooked.	Madeira....................1 glassful.
Butter............3 tablespoonsful.	Milk.......................1 pint.
Flour............3 tablespoonsful.	Stock or water...........2 quarts.

Time.—1 hour.

PREPARATION.—1st. Take the flesh off the tail and the claws, slice it and put it apart. 2d. Break fine in a mortar the shells and claws with 3 tablespoonsful butter. 3d. Put that pap in a sauce pan with 1 glassful madeira, let it cook a while, add 3 tablespoonsful flour, stir well the whole, add 1 pint milk and let boil a while. 4th. Sift the whole through a strainer, put this pap in a sauce pan, add 2 quarts stock or water, let warm well and when ready to serve add the juice of a lemon, some cayenne pepper, and 2 tablespoonsful butter. 5th. Place the slices of flesh in a tureen, pour the soup over and serve hot.

RECAPITULATION.

I. FAT SOUP. CLEAR.

1. Bouillon.
2. Consomme......................Fundament of other soups.
3. Consomme de volaille...........Consomme of fowl.
4. Pot au feu.......... ....⎫
5. Croute au pot.................. . ⎬ Stock or consomme with vegetables previously cooked apart in some boiling water.
6. Printanier......................... ⎬
7. Brunoise........... .... ⎭
8. Julienne .... ⎱ Stock or consomme with vegetables not having been cooked as above.
9. Colbert ....Printanier with poached eggs.
10. Consomme au riz............... ⎫
11. Consomme au vermicelle..... ⎬ Stock or consomme with farinaceous substances, having been previously cooked apart, in boiling water.
12. Consomme au macaroni...... ⎭
13. Potage milanaise .... ⎱ Consomme or stock with macaroni and rasped cheese.

II. FAT SOUPS. HALF THICK.

14. Ox tail............................. ⎱ Stock with madeira, starch and pieces of oxtail or calf's head.
15. Potage tortue .... ⎰
16. Mullagatawny .... ⎱ Stock with flour and flesh, beef in the former and fowl in the second.
17. Tchy a la Russe................. ⎰
18. Potage Semoule Liee............Stock with semolia, eggs and cream.
19. Potage a l'orge....................Stock with barley, cream, butter.
20. Potage Andaloux.
21. Borch a la Polonaise.............Beets, milk and stock.

III. FAT SOUP. PUREE OR CREAM.

22. Potage a la Reine.........Cream of fowl.....................⎫
23. Creme de Celeri...........Cream of celery................ ⎬
24. Creme d'asperges.........Cream of asparagus............ ⎬ Always prepared with stock.
25. Creme de choux fleurs..Cream of cauliflower .... ⎬
26. Puree Crecy........ ....Cream of carrots with rice.. ⎭
27. *Potage St. Germain... ....Cream of green peas.
28. *Potage Conde ....Cream of white kidney beans.
29. *Potage Musard ....Cream of red kidney beans.
30. *Creme de Lentilles...............Cream of lentils

I. LEAN SOUP. CLEAR.

31. Potage Paysanne.
32. Soupe a l'onion.
33. Soupe a l'oseille ....Sorrel soup.
34. Ouka de perches a la Russe...Fish soup.
35. Bouillabaisse ....Highly seasoned fish soup.
36. Soupe aux huitres.................Oyster soup.
37. Soupe aux clams.

* May be prepared with water instead of stock for a lean dinner.

II. LEAN SOUPS. HALF THICK.

38. Potage velour......................Soup with starch, eggs and butter.
20. Potage andaloux...................Lean or fat.
39. Potage Parmentier................Cream of potatoes.
40. Semoule au lait ....Semolia with milk.

III. LEAN SOUP. PUREE OR CREAM.

41. Potage Princesse ....Puree of bread..............
27. Potage St. Germain ....Cream of green peas ....
28. Potage Conde .... Cream of white kidney beans
29. Potage Musard ....Cream of red kidney beans
30. Creme de lentilles..................Cream of lentils.... ....
42. Creme de poturons ....Cream of pumpkins...........
43. Creme de mais ....Cream of sweet corn..........
44. Creme Duchesse Buckingham Cream of almonds ....
45. Bisque de homards ....Cream of lobsters ....

Lean or fat.

PUREES OR CREAM.

GENERAL REMARKS.

The puree or cream is quite a thick soup, very palatable and substantial. It is made out of fowl, game, vegetables, or fish. In every case you have first to cook well the particular materials until tender and to sift them through a sifter to obtain quite a clear pap; to which you add what the French cooks call a "liaison," *binding*, to unite all the parts together. This is made with yolks, cream and butter (also sometimes flour or starch), and *don't forget*

1st. That this "liaison" should be added only when ready to serve.

2d. That the sauce pan shall be placed on a corner of the range and that you should add some of the hot pap to your "liaison" before you pour it in the sauce pan.

3d. That you should never allow a soup to boil after you have poured in a "liaison."

THE

HORS D'OEUVRES

The hors d'oeuvres are to be served more often at lunches than at dinners; however a quite fashionable dinner cannot be without some of them, at least without some cold ones. The "hors d'oeuvres" are divided into cold and warm, the former being more common because they are more easily prepared.

THE COLD HORS D'OEUVRES.

Usually the cold *hors d'oeuvres* are placed on the table in advance; by so doing you add to the general decorative effect and the guests will find at their disposal some light dishes, as soon as they have finished their soup and while awaiting the fish.

They should always be served in special dishes (radish dish, relish dishes, butter boat, etc.) in china or crystal.

46. RADISHES.

They should be young and fresh. Cut the end of the root and leave only enough of the leaves to permit of taking them easily with the fingers.

47. OLIVES.

Should be very green and served on a relish boat.

48. SARDINES.

Should be taken from the box just before serving and disposed gently on a relish dish with some of their oil poured over.

49. ANCHOVIES.

Serve as in the case of sardines.

50. SMOKED OR DRIED MEAT OR FISH.

Should be sliced very fine and the slices disposed in a circle with some parsley in the middle.

51. CUCUMBER SALAD.

Pare and slice the cucumbers, pour some salt over them, to facilitate the disengagement of the juice. After 10 min. drip those slices and mix with some pepper, oil and vinegar.

52. TOMATO SALAD.

Prepare as the above, but don't peel them.

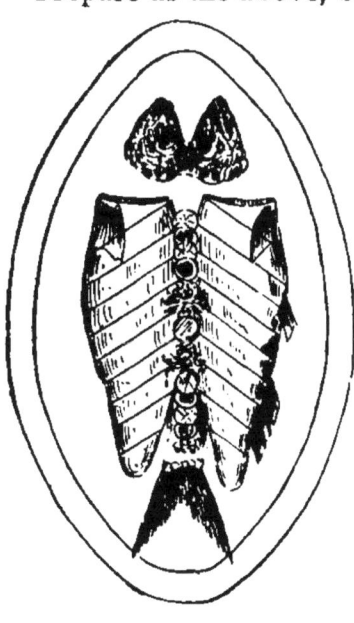

53. HERRINGS.

1st. SMOKED.—Cut them in the middle, take the back bone and the skin off, cut the fillets in pieces 1 inch wide, dispose upon a plate and pour some olive oil over them. 2d. SALTED.—They should be freshened for 2 days in half milk and half water, then cut in the middle, take off the back bone, cut the fillets in pieces 1 inch wide and arrange them on a plate according to the accompanying cut. Pour over some oil mixed with vinegar, then chop apart the yolk and the white of a hard egg, also some parsley and red beets and dispose between the two halves.

54. OYSTERS.

Should be opened before serving and presented on the hollow shell and not on the flat one, serve with lemons cut in two or four and not with vinegar.

WARM HORS D'OEUVRES.

The warm hors d'oeuvres belong more to the "Restaurant" than to the "Family" cooking. However the following are quite simple to prepare and will have a nice effect with a fashionable dinner.

They should be served when the guests are finishing their soup and be cooked just before serving. Therefore it is difficult to serve them when you have more than 8 or 10 guests, and we recommend them more for select lunch and tea parties than for regular dinners.

55. CROQUETTES VOLAILLE.

CROQUETTES OF FOWL.

NOTE.—The flesh of fowls having served to make the stock (see foot note 1) is advantageously employed for croquettes.

PROPORTIONS:

Fowl ....The flesh of one.	Parsley ....
Yolks...............2.	Mushrooms........ }A small amount.
Stock ....2 glassesful.	Truffles.............
Butter ....2 tablespoonsful	Bread crumbs.....Enough to roll the
Eggs... ....1 or 2	croquettes in.
Flour...............2 tablespoonsful.	

PREPARATION.—1st. Remove the flesh, chop it fine, chop also the mushrooms, the parsley and the truffles, mix all together. 2d. Let melt in a sauce pan 2 tablespoonsful butter mixed with 2 tablespoonsful flour, add little by little and while stirring about 2 glassesful of stock, let boil awhile in stirring till this sauce becomes a little thick. 3d. Add the chopped flesh, etc , stir well the whole and add two yolks, stir again till well mixed. 4th. Pour in a dish so as to obtain a coat 1 inch thick, let cool, taking care to place some buttered paper over to prevent the upper part from drying and becoming black. 5th. When cold, cut in pieces about two inches long and 1 inch wide, roll them in some flour, dip them in a beaten egg, roll them again in some bread crumbs. 6th. Let fry in butter, serve on a folded napkin.

56. FILLETS DE VOLAILLE.

FILLETS OF FOWL.

PROPORTIONS:

Fowl..2 young chickens.
Flour......................................2 tablespoonsful.
Milk ....1 glassful.
Bread crumbs ....Enough to roll the fillets in.
Butter............ ....Enough to fry the fillets.
Time.—½ hour.

PREPARATION.—1st. Take the fillets and the legs off, cut the fillets in 2 and the legs in 3 2d. Dip those pieces in some milk, roll them in flour or bread chipping and fry in butter.

NOTE.—Use the bodies of the chicken when making stock.

57. HUITRES FRITTES.

Fried oysters. See oysters No. 145.

58. HUITRES GRILLEES.

Broiled oysters. See oysters No. 146.

59. COQUILLES DE SAUMON A LA PARISIENNE.

See No. 82.

60. COQUILLES DE TRUITE.

See No. 82.

61. COQUILLES DE PIKE.

See No. 82.

62. COQUILLES DE HOMARD.

See No. 139.

63. COTELETTES DE HOMARD.

See No. 138.

64. SOUFFLET AU FROMAGE.

PROPORTIONS.—For five persons:

Cheese .... ½ lb. (Swiss or   Milk..................... 2 glassesful.
                 Parmesan.)   Flour .... 2 tablespoonsful.
Eggs................. 3.   Small paper boxes. 10.

Time.—1 hour.

PREPARATION.—1st. Break 3 eggs, put the yolks in a sauce pan and the whites apart. 2d. Add in the sauce pan a little salt and white pepper, 2 spoonsful of flour, stir well the whole, add 2 glassesful of milk, let cook while stirring for ¼ hour. 3d. Add ½ lb. rasped cheese (Swiss or Parmesan). 4th. The above being well mixed, put the sauce pan on a corner of the range, beat your white of egg, a salad dish is very convenient for that purpose* and add the beaten eggs little by little, while stirring. 5th. Fill your paper boxes ¾ full, put them on a baking plate, let bake in an oven until well risen and until the soufflet becomes bright yellow. Serve immediately.

---

* Never beat whites except in earthenware, glass or *copper* utensils.

65. RAMKINS.

PROPORTIONS.—For five persons:

Eggs ....4.   Cheese..⅓ lb. (Parmesan or Swiss.)
Flour ....3 spoonsful.   Water...1 glassful.
Butter.....................3 spoonsful.

PREPARATION.—1st. In a sauce pan, put 1 glass water, 3 tablespoonsful butter, let boil and add while stirring and little by little about 3 tablespoonsful of flour. 2d. When the mass is thick enough let it cool a little on a corner of the range and add 4 eggs, one by one, while beating continually. 3d. Add 6 oz. rasped cheese, stir well and put this pap on a pie plate, in the shape of small cakes about an inch distant, and sprinkle over 2 oz. cheese cut in very small dices. Let bake in an oven till light brown.

66. HARENGS EN PAPILLOTTE.

PROPORTIONS.—For five persons:

Herring, salted..............3.   Parsley.........½ handful.
Mushrooms..................¼ lb.   Flour...........1 tablespoonful.
Onions..........................1.   Stock..........1 glassful.

Time.—½ hour.

PREPARATION.—1st. Freshen 3 salted herring (53). 2d. Skin them, take the fillets off and divide them in two. 3d. Make a "sauce papillotte" as follows: Fry in butter till light brown 1 chopped onion, add ¼ lb. box mushrooms, ½ handful parsley, 1 fillet, all chopped fine, 1 tablespoonful flour, 1 glass bouillon, let cook awhile.

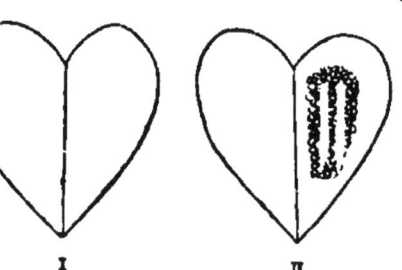

I   II   III

4th. Cut 10 pieces paper according to the figure No. 1, butter them, put 1 tablespoonful "papillote" sauce on one half, then ½ fillets, then another spoonful sauce. 5th. Fold this paper in two, close the edges, put those "papillottes" on a pie plate, let bake awhile and serve in crown on a dish.

RECAPITULATION.

COLD HORS D'OEUVRES	*46 Radishes.	
	*47 Olives.	
	*48 Sardines.	
	*49 Anchovies.	
	50 Smoked or dried meat or fish.*	
	*51 Cucumber salad.	
	*52 Tomato salad.	
	*53 Herrings. 53a. Smoked. 53b. Salted.	
	*54 Oysters.	
WARM HORS D'OEUVRES	55 Croquettes de Volaille....................Croquettes of fowl.	
	56 Fillets de Volaille...........................Fillets of fowl.	
	57 Huitres Frittes...............................Fried oysters.	
	58 Huitres Grillées.............................Broiled oysters.	
	59 Coquilles de Saumon à la Parisienne.Salmon.	
	60 Coquilles de Truite à la Parisienne...Trout.	
	61 Coquilles de Pike à la Parisienne......Pike.	
	62 Coquilles de Homard à la Parisienne..Lobsters.	
	63 Cotelettes de Homard ....Lobster Cutlets.	
	*64 Soufflet au Fromage........................	
	*65 Ramkins	
	*66 Harengs en Papillotte....................	

* Lean.

FISH
AND
SHELL FISH.

There is certainly a greater number of fish in the United States than we have mentioned in this chapter, but having selected the most typical and common and having given for each the most appropriate mode of preparation and sauces, we think we have enabled the house-wife to prepare, by analogy, any fish she may wish to handle.

Don't forget above all, that the first quality of a fish is its freshness, and to be fresh a fish should have these qualities:

1st. Its flesh thick and firm.   2d. Its eyes full and prominent.

3d. Its scales or gills bright.

SALMON AND TROUT.

67. SAUMON OR TRUITE AU COURT BOUILLON.

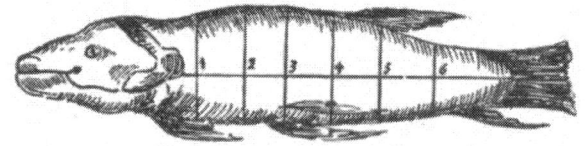

BOILED SALMON OR TROUT.

67a Sauce Hollandaise.   67b Sauce aux Capres (Caper Sauce.)

67c Sauce Polonaise.

NOTE.—According to the number of the guests you serve a whole salmon or a part of it; a family dinner of 5 will require about 3 to 4 lbs. of fish, and we recommend to cook the same entire instead of slicing before cooking.

TROUT.—The trout and especially the salmon trout having very great analogy to the salmon, what is said for the latter may be applied to the former.

The fishes cooked "au court bouillon" being served with the sauce apart, we recommend cooking about twice as much fish as the dinner requires, because the remainder may be kept fresh for some days in an ice box and served cold as indicated in No. 81.

PREPARATION.—We will tell here how to cook a whole salmon, from about 8 to 10 lbs. and it will be exactly the same with any other fish or part of fish to be cooked "au court bouillon." 1st. Clean and wash your fish, remove the gills and the fins, but preserve the tail, place the fish in a fish kettle (with a grate in the bottom so as not to break it, when you take it from the kettle) with 2 carrots, 1 onion sliced, some thyme and laurel, 6 grains of whole pepper and enough water to cover the fish well. 2d. Let heat and *as soon as it boils* place the fish pan on a corner of the stove and let simmer for about 1 hour without letting boil. 3d. Serve in a long dish on a folded napkin and dispose around the fish or serve apart 2 nice potatoes for each guest, boiled in slightly salted water and carefully carved. Serve the sauce apart. For the sauces see Nos. 151-152-159.

68. SAUMON OR TRUITE AU BLEU.

SAUCE GENEVOISE.

PREPARATION.—Same as for the above but cook the fish in half water and half red wine instead of pure water. For the sauce see No. 158.

69. SAUMON OR TRUITE AU BLANC.

69a Sauce aux Huitres.
69b Sauce Cardinal.
69c Sauce Homard.
69d Sauce Crevette.

PREPARATION.—Same as for the above but use white wine instead of red wine. For the sauces see Nos. 153-154-155-156.

70. TRUITE AU VIN BLANC.

PROPORTIONS.—For five persons:

Trout............4 to 5 lbs.
Flour... ....3 tablespoonsful.
Butter............5 tablespoonsful.
Yolks ....2.

Stock...............2 glassesful.
White wine......2 glassesful.
Vegetables........1 onion, 1 carrot, some thyme and laurel.

Time.—1 hour.

PREPARATION.—1st.　Clean and wash your fish, remove the gills, place it in a fish kettle with 1 tablespoonful of butter, 2 glassesful of stock, 2 glassesful of white wine, 1 onion and 1 carrot sliced, some thyme and laurel; allow to cook slowly for about ½ hour while basting from time to time.　2d.　When ready to serve, skin the fish carefully, and place it in a long dish.　3d.　Pass through a sifter the juice of the fish and the vegetables, pour this pap in a sauce pan where you have melted 2 tablespoonsful of butter with 3 tablespoonsful of flour and let boil awhile while stirring.　4th.　When ready to serve place the sauce pan on a corner of the range, mix in a bowl 2 tablespoonsful of butter with two yolks, add little by little some of the sauce while beating, and pour into the sauce pan while stirring.　Don't allow the sauce to boil again and pour it over the fish which you serve with potatoes (as indicated in No. 67).

71. TRUITE AU GRATIN.

PROPORTIONS.—For five persons:

Trout, 5 to 6 lbs....1.	Onion...............1.
Butter.................5 tablespoonsful.	Parsley..............¼ handful.
White wine..........2 glassesful.	Bread chipping...1 tablespoonful.

Time.—½ to ¾ hour.

PREPARATION.—1st.　Clean, wash, etc., your trout, place it on a long dish, and place in different places on its back about 1 tablespoonful of butter.　2d.　Let brown (clear brown) in a sauce pan 1 chopped onion in 1 tablespoonful butter, then add 2 glassesful white wine, ¼ handful hashed parsley, let boil awhile and pour the sauce over the fish.　3d.　Sprinkle over some bread crumbs, pour over about 2 tablespoonsful melted butter and let cook slowly in an oven for about ¼ hour.　Serve with potatoes apart (as indicated in No. 67).

72. SAUMON GRILLE.

BROILED SALMON.

72a Maitre d'hôtel.	72c Sauce Tartare.
72b Sauce Mayonnaise.	72d Sauce Remoulade.

PROPORTIONS.—For five persons:

Salmon..3 steaks, about 1 lb. each.	Lemon.................1, cut in 6 pieces.
Olive oil..2 tablespoonsful.	Salt and pepper...To suit the taste.

Time.—½ hour.

PREPARATION.—Place the steaks in a hollow plate, sprinkle over some salt and pepper, and also a little olive oil, turn them twice or three times and let broil on a moderate fire taking care to turn the slices from time to time. 2d. Sprinkle over the juice of ⅛ of the lemon and serve with a maitre d'hôtel or one of the above mentioned sauces separately, and also with a lemon cut in 6 pieces. For the sauces see Nos. 161-162-163-164.

73. PETITES TRUITES A LA MEUNIERE.

BROOK TROUT FRIED A LA MEUNIERE.

PROPORTIONS.—For five persons:

Brook trout....From 5 to 10.	Butter....................¼ lb.
Flour.. ....2 to 4 tablespoonsful.	Hashed parsley.......1 tablespoonful.
Milk.............About 2 glassesful.	Lemon ....1.

Time.—½ hour.

PREPARATION.—1st. Clean and wash your trouts, dip them in some milk (placed in a soup plate), roll them in flour and let them fry slowly for about ¼ hour in ¼ lb. butter (very fresh) taking care to turn them often and not to allow the butter to become black. 2d. Serve on a *warm* dish, sprinkle over some hashed parsley, press over the juice of a lemon and pour over them the butter in which they have been fried.

74. FILLETS DE TRUITE A LA COLBERT.

FRIED FILLETS OF TROUT A LA COLBERT.

PROPORTIONS.—For five persons:

Trout......4 to 5 lbs.	Parsley ....½ handful.
Milk.......About 2 glassesful.	Lard or fat.........Enough to fry.
Flour......3 tablespoonsful.	Lemon..............1.

Time.—½ hour.

PREPARATION.—1st. Clean and wash the trout, remove the fillets, cut them in 3 parts, dip in milk and roll in flour as for No. 73, and let fry in fat or lard till well colored.* 2d. Serve on a folded napkin with ½ handful parsley fried in the same lard after the fish, and also with a lemon cut in 5 parts.

75. FILLETS DE TRUITE AU GRATIN.

FILLETS OF TROUT AU GRATIN.

PROPORTIONS.—For five persons:

Trout...............2 of about 3 lbs. each.	White wine.........1 glassful.
Butter...............5 tablespoonsful.	Hashed parsley...1 tablespoonful.
	Bread crumbs......1 tablespoonful.

Time.—¼ hour.

---

*The heat of the fat should get such a degree that when a little piece of bread is dropped in it, it will become brown instantly, but it should not be so hot as to burn the fat.

PREPARATION.—lst. Clean and wash the trout, take off the fillets, cut them in 3 parts and dispose them on a buttered dish. 2d.   Pour over 1 glassful white wine, some hashed parsley and some bread crumbs, some salt and pepper, about 3 tablespoonsful butter distributed in different places, and let the fish bake in an oven until it becomes a clear brown.

76. FILLETS DE TRUITE AU VIN BLANC.

FILLETS OF TROUT WITH WHITE WINE.

PROPORTIONS.—For five persons:

Trout ....2 of about 3 lbs. each.	Flour...................1 tablespoonful.
	Onion...................1.
Butter.................5 tablespoonsful.	Hashed parsley.....1 tablespoonful.
White wine ....2 glassesful.	Salt and pepper.....A little.

Time.—¾ hour.

PREPARATION.—lst.   Clean and wash the trout, remove the fillets, pare them and put them on a buttered dish. 2d.   Let bake for about 10 minutes in an oven (to solidify them). 3d.   Let cook awhile in a sauce pan 1 chopped onion with 1 tablespoonful of butter, add 1 tablespoonful of flour, sprinkle over some hashed parsley, some salt and pepper, add 2 glassesful white wine, let boil awhile, then add two tablespoonsful fine butter.   4th.   Pour this sauce over the fillets and let bake for ¼ hour.

77. FILLETS DE TRUITE NORMANDE.

FILLETS OF TROUT NORMANDE.

(For fine dinners.)

PROPORTIONS.—For five persons:

Trout ....About 6 lbs.	Stock .... 1 glassful.
Vegetables.......1 carrot, 1 onion, ⅓ celery stalk, some thyme and laurel.	White wine.......... 2 glassesful.
	Mushrooms..........12.
	Oysters................12.
Yolks ....2.	Mussels................24.
Butter ....4 tablespoonsful.	Shrimps...............24.
Flour...............4 tablespoonsful.	Small pieces toast..12.

Time.—1¼ hours.

PREPARATION.—lst and 2d.   As above in No. 76. 3d.   Put the heads, bones, and parings of the fillets in a kettle with about 1 quart water, 1 onion, 1 carrot, ⅓ celery stalk sliced, some thyme and laurel, 1 glass bouillon and 2 glasses white wine, allow to cook for about ⅓ hour.   4th.   Dispose with taste on or around your fillets the following garnishes: 12 *mushrooms,* canned or previously cooked in some boiling water, 24 shrimps tails, 12 oysters taken from their shells and boiled a little while in their own juice (this juice should be preserved), 24 mussels cooked for 5 min. in their shells and then removed (their juice should be preserved), 12 small pieces of toast fried in butter. 5th. Make a sauce Normande as follows: Let melt in a sauce pan 2 tablespoonsful butter mixed with 4 tablespoonsful flour, add the juice of the fillets, the oysters and the mussels, and also the fish stock (3rd) passed through a strainer or a sifter, stir well the whole, then beat in a bowl 2 yolks with some of this sauce, put the sauce pan on a corner of the range, pour in the contents of the bowl and then pour the sauce over the fillets. 6th. Let bake in an oven from 5 to 10 min. and serve with potatoes apart (No. 67).

78. FILLETS DE TRUITE A LA CREME

FILLETS OF TROUT WITH CREAM.

PROPORTIONS.—For five persons:

Trout	4 to 5 lbs.	Milk	3 pints.
Butter	4 tablespoonsful.	Salt and white pepper	A little.
Flour	2 tablespoonsful.	*Time.*—¾ hour to 1 hour.	

PREPARATION.—1st. and 2d. Same as for No. 76. 3d. Let melt in a sauce pan 2 tablespoonsful butter mixed with 2 tablespoonsful flour, then add 3 pints milk, some salt and white pepper, let boil awhile and pour this sauce over the fillets. 4th. Let bake in an oven till clear brown.

79. FILLETS DE TRUITE A LA TANTY.

FILLETS OF TROUT A LA TANTY.

(For great dinners or banquets.)

PROPORTIONS.—For five persons:

Trout	4 to 5 lbs.	Flour	3 tablespoonsful.
Lobster	2 to 3 lbs.	Milk	1 quart.
Butter	¾ lb.	Carmine	A little.
	Time.—1 hour.		

PREPARATION.— 1st and 2d. Same as No. 76. 3d. Take the flesh and the tail and the claws of the lobster, slice it and dispose these slices on or around the fillets. 4th. Make a sauce "Tanty" as follows: Let melt in a sauce pan ¼ lb. butter, mixed with 3 tablespoonsful flour, add little by little and while stirring 1 quart milk, some salt and pepper and the paws and shells of the lobsters broken fine in a mortar, some salt and white pepper, add also a little bit carmine (this is to give nice flavor and fine rose color). 5th. Let boil for 5 minutes, pass the whole through a sifter and pour this sauce on the fillets. Let bake for 10 minutes and serve with potatoes (No. 67).

80. SAUMON FROID OR TRUITE FROIDE, A L'IMPERIALE.

Cold Salmon, Cold Trout, a l'Imperiale.

Note.—Always served entire.

Proportions.—We give here the proportions for a 6 to 8 lb. trout to be served at a dinner for 10 persons:

Trout ....6 to 8 lbs.
Vegetables...Green peas, green kidney beans, carrots cut in dices, carved cauliflowers, about 3 tablespoonsful of each.
Salad.....................1 handful.   Parsley...................1 handful.

Preparation.—1st. Cook a trout "au court bouillon" (No. 67) and let it cool in the water in which it has been cooked.   2d.   When cold, let it drip, skin carefully and place in a folded napkin on a long dish.   3d.   Cook in boiling water and separately some green kidney beans, green peas, carrots cut in dices, cauliflowers carved in balls about the size of a hazel nut, season them separately with salt, pepper, oil and vinegar and dispose them with taste in small cakes around the fish with some green salad leaves and parsley wisps.   Serve with a sauce mayonnaise or sauce tartare apart.   For the sauces see Nos. 162-163.

81. SAUMON FROID OR TRUITE FROIDE.

81a Sauce Mayonnaise.   81c Sauce Remoulade.
81b Sauce Tartare.   81d Sauce Vinaigrette.

Preparation.—Let cool a salmon or trout boiled "au court bouillon" or serve what is left over from a fish cooked in the same manner with the sauce apart.   For the sauces see Nos. 162-163-164-165.

82. COQUILLES DE SAUMON OR COQUILLES DE TRUITE

A LA CALIFORNIENNE.

Note.—These are made out of cold salmon, trout, pike, etc., remaining from fishes previously served "au court bouillon," "au bleu" or "au blanc," and are served in quite large flat shells, "coquilles" in French.   They are very convenient for lunch or tea parties.

Proportions.—For five persons:

Cold fish........1 to 2 lbs.   Stock...................1 glassful.
Butter............5 tablespoonsful. White wine..........2 glassesful.
Flour.............2 tablespoonsful. Yolks..................2.
Bread crumbs..2 tablespoonsful.   Onion...................1.
Rasped cheese.1 tablespoonful.   *Time.*—¾ hour.

PREPARATION.—1st. Divide the flesh of the fish in quite small pieces. 2d. Let brown in a sauce pan 1 chopped onion with 1 tablespoonful butter, sprinkle over 2 tablespoonsful flour, add 1 glassful stock and 2 glassesful white wine, some salt and pepper. 3d. Beat in a bowl 2 yolks with 2 tablespoonsful butter, add some of the sauce, pour the whole in the sauce pan (*don't allow to boil again*), add the divided fish, stir well the whole and place upon 10 flat shells. 5th. Sprinkle over some bread crumbs, some rasped cheese (Parmesan or Swiss), pour over 2 tablespoonsful melted butter and let bake in an oven for 5 minutes. Serve on a folded napkin.

PIKE.

83. PIKE AU COURT BOUILLON.

BOILED PIKE.

83a Sauce Hollandaise.   83b Sauce aux Capres.
            83c Sauce Polonaise.
As for the Truite au Court Bouillon, No. 67.

84. PIKE AU BLEU.

Sauce Genevoise.
As for the Truite au Bleu, No. 68.

85. PIKE AU BLANC.

85a Sauce aux Huitres   85c Sauce Homard.
85b Sauce Cardinal.   85d Sauce Crevettes.
As for the Truite au Blanc, No. 69.

86. PIKE AU VIN BLANC.

PIKE WITH WHITE WINE.

As for the Truite au vin Blanc, No. 70.

87. PIKE AU GRATIN.

As for the Truite au Gratin, No. 71.

88. FILLETS DE PIKE FRITS A LA COLBERT.

FRIED FILLETS OF PIKE A LA COLBERT.

As for the Fillets Truite a la Colbert, No. 74.

89. FILLETS DE PIKE AU GRATIN.

As for the Fillets Truite au Gratin, No. 75.

90. FILLETS DE PIKE AU VIN BLANC.

As for the Fillets de Truite au vin Blanc, No. 76.

91. FILLETS DE PIKE NORMANDE.

As for the Fillets de Truite Normande, No. 77.

92. FILLETS DE PIKE A LA CREME.

As for the Fillets de Truite a la Creme, No. 78.

93. FILLETS DE PIKE A LA TANTY.

As for the Fillets de Truite a la Tanty, No. 79.

94. PIKE FROID A L'IMPERIALE.

As for the Truite Froide a l'Imperiale, No. 80.

95. PIKE FROID.

95a Sauce Mayonnaise.   95c Sauce Remoulade.
95b Sauce Tartare.   95d Sauce Vinaigrette.

As for the Truite Froide, No. 81.

96. COQUILLES DE PIKE CALIFORNIENNE.

As for the Coquilles de Truite, No. 82.

PICKEREL.

97. BROCHET AU BLEU SAUCE GENEVOISE.

(BROCHET IS FRENCH FOR PICKEREL.)

As for the Truite au Bleu, No. 68.

98. BROCHET A LA JUIVE.

PICKEREL, JEWISH STYLE.

PROPORTIONS:

Pickerel.........1 of 5 to 6 lbs.	Butter..............½ lb.
Onions..........3 to 4.	Stock...............1 glassful.
Parsley..........1 handful.	White wine ......1 pint.

Time.—¾ hour.

PREPARATION.—1st. Clean and wash the pike, place it in a fish kettle (somewhat larger than the fish), with 3 to 4 sliced onions, 1 handful parsley, ¼ lb. butter, 1 pint white wine, 1 glassful stock, some salt and pepper, put the cover on and let cook slowly while basting for about ½ hour. 2d. Take the fish with care from the kettle, and place carefully on a warm dish, then add while stirring about ¼ lb. fresh butter to the sauce and pour it over the fish.

99. BROCHET FROID.

COLD PICKEREL.

99a Sauce Mayonnaise.   99b Sauce Tartare.
99c Sauce Vinaigrette.

As for the Truite Froide, No. 81.

CARP.

100. CARPE AU BLEU.

As for the Truite au Bleu, No. 68.

101. CARPE A LA JUIVE.

CARP JEWISH STYLE.

As for Brochet a la Juive, No. 98.

102. CARPE FRITTE.

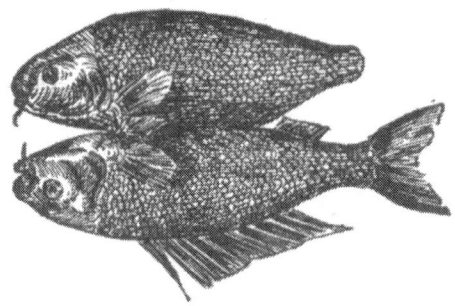

FRIED CARP.

Take carp of medium size, clean and wash carefully, cut them in two (in length), and do as indicated for the Fillets a la Colbert, No. 74.

103. CARPES EN MATELOTTE.

Do as indicated for the "Matelotte Marinière" No. 106, and use about 6 lbs. carp.*

*We recommend, when possible, to make the matelotte out of several kinds of fish as pike, pickerel, carp, eel., etc.

EEL.

104. ANGUILLES GRILLES.

Broiled Eels, Sauce Tartare.

PROPORTIONS.—

Eels...........3 to 4 lbs.
Butter........4 tablespoonsful.
Vinegar......1 glassful.

Vegetables.....1 onion, 1 carrot,
thyme and laurel.
Time.—¾ hour.

PREPARATION.—1st. Clean and wash your eels, take the skin off and cut in pieces about 3 inches long. 2d. Put them in a sauce pan with about 2 quarts *cold* water, 1 glassful vinegar, 1 onion and 1 carrot sliced, some thyme and laurel, salt and pepper, let them boil, place the kettle on a corner of the range and let simmer for about ¼ hour. 3d. Let drip the pieces on a folded napkin, dip them in melted butter (placed in a warm soup dish), roll them in bread crumbs and broil on light fire by turning from time to time. Serve with a tartare sauce, No 163.

105. MATELOTTE D'ANGUILLES.

Do as indicated below for the "Matelotte a la Marinière." (No. 106.)*

106. MATELOTTE A LA MARINIERE.

PROPORTIONS.—For five persons:

Fish...... ....Pike, pickerel, carp, eels, about 6 lbs. in all.
Onions. ....12.
Small cloves....3.
Mushrooms ....¼ lb.
Red wine........ 1 quart.

Butter.............¼ lb.
Flour..............2 tablespoonsful.
Toasts.............
Salt and pepper
Time.—½ hour.

PREPARATION.—1st. Clean and wash your fish, cut them in pieces 3 inches long, place them in a sauce pan with 3 cloves, 12 small onions, ½ lb. mushrooms (if canned don't put the juice in), and some salt and pepper; cover with red wine. 2d. Let boil quickly on hot fire for 5 minutes, then place the pan on a corner of the range and add ¼ lb. butter mixed with 2 tablespoonsful of flour. 3d. Let cook the whole slowly and without allowing to boil for about 5 minutes till the sauce becomes a little thick. Serve on a warm hollow dish with some toasts fried in butter.

---

* We recommend, when possible, to make the matellotte out of several kinds of fish as pike, pickerel, carp, eel, etc.

BLACK BASS.

107. BLACK BASS AUX FINES HERBES.

NOTE.—For black bass of 4 lbs. and over.

PROPORTIONS.—

Black bass...1 of from 5 to 6 lbs.	Hashed parsley..................1.
Butter.........4 tablespoonsful.	Lemon ....1.

Time.—⅓ hour.

PREPARATION.—1st. Clean and wash the fish, place it on the lower grate of the fish kettle and dip it in boiling salted water, keep boiling for 10 to 15 minutes according to the size. 2d. Drip the fish, place it on a warm dish, sprinkle over the juice of a lemon and 2 tablespoonsful melted butter mixed with 1 tablespoonful hashed parsley. Serve with potatoes. (As in No 67.)

108. BLACK BASS GRILLE.

BROILED BLACK BASS.

PROPORTIONS.—For five persons:

Black bass.....2 of about 3 lbs. each.	Salt and pepper...To suit the taste.
Olive oil ......2 tablespoonsful.	*Time.*—⅓ hour.

PREPARATION.—1st. Clean and wash the fish, divide them in two parts (lengthwise), place those halves on a dish and sprinkle over some salt and pepper, and also 2 tablespoonsful of olive oil to prevent the fish clinging to the broiler; turn them 2 or 3 times. 2d. Let broil as indicated in No. 72.

109. BLACK BASS FRIT.

FRIED BLACK BASS.

PROPORTIONS.—

Black Bass.....2, of about 3 lbs. each.	Hashed parsley......1 tablespoonful.
Milk.............2 glassesful.	Lemon...................1.
Flour............2 tablespoonsful.	*Time*—½ hour.

PREPARATION.—1st. As 1st. in No. 108. 2d. As for the Fillets de Truite a la Colbert (No. 74).

SHAD.

110. ALOSE GRILLEE.

BROILED SHAD.

110a Maitre d'Hôtel.	110c Sauce Tartare.
110b Sauce Mayonnaise.	110d Sauce Remoulade.

PROPORTIONS.—

Shad..............1, of about 4 lbs.	Salt and pepper.....To suit the taste.
Oil................2 tablespoonsful.	*Time*—⅓ hour.

PREPARATION.—1st   Clean and wash the shad, notch the flancs (the notches should be about 2 inches distant and ⅛ inch deep), so that the inside may cook as well as the outside, place the shad on a dish, sprinkle over some salt and pepper, and 2 tablespoonsful olive oil.   2d.   Let broil, taking care to turn the fish from time to time to cook it uniformly.   For the sauces see Nos. 161, 162, 163, 164.

111. OEUFS D'ALOSE GRILLES.

BROILED SHAD'S ROE.

PROPORTIONS.—For five persons:

Shad roe...........About 1½ lbs.	Butter ....¼ lb.
Olive oil...........2 tablespoonsful.	Hashed parsley.1 tablespoonful.
Salt and pepper..To suit the taste.	*Time.*—¼ hour.

PREPARATION.—1st.   Handle the roe very carefully so as not to break the skin which unites the eggs.   Sprinkle over, as indicated above, olive oil, let broil and serve with a maitre d'hôtel; that is to say with ¼ lb. fresh butter mixed with 1 tablespoonful hashed parsley with which you cover the eggs as soon as they have been placed on the dish (warm); this butter shall melt on the eggs.

RED SNAPPER.

112. RED SNAPPER GRILLE.

BROILED RED SNAPPER.

112a Maitre d'Hôtel.	112c Sauce Tartare.
112b Sauce Mayonnaise.	112d Sauce Provencale.

As for the Alose Grillee, No. 110.   For the sauces, No. 161, 162, 163, 164.

WHITEFISH.

113. WHITEFISH GRILLE.

BROILED WHITEFISH.

113a Maitre d'Hôtel.	113c Sauce Tartare.
113b Sauce Mayonnaise.	113d Sauce Remoulade.

As for the Black Bass Grille, No. 108.

SOLLE.

114. SOLLE FRITTE.

FRIED SOLE.

As for the Fillets de Truite a la Colbert, No. 74, but the fish to be fried entire.

115. FILLETS DE SOLLE TRUITE A LA COLBERT.

As for the Fillets de Truite a la Colbert, No. 74.

116. FILLETS DE SOLLE AU GRATIN.

As for the Fillets de Truite au Gratin, No. 75.

117. FILLETS DE SOLLE AU VIN BLANC.

As for the Fillets de Truite au vin Blanc, No. 76.

118. FILLETS DE SOLLE NORMANDE.

As for the Fillets de Truite Normande, No. 77.

119. FILLETS DE SOLLE A LA CREME.

As for the Fillets de Truite a la Creme, No. 78.

120. FILLETS DE SOLLE A LA TANTY.

As for the Fillets de Truite a la Tanty, No. 79.

MACKEREL.

121. MAQUEREAU GRILLE MAITRE DE HOTEL.

BROILED MACKEREL.

As for the Whitefish Grille, No. 113.

WHITING.

122. MERLANS FRITS.

FRIED WHITING.

As for the Fillets de Truite a la Colbert, No. 74, but fry the fish whole.

123. MERLANS AU VIN BLANC.

WHITING WITH WHITE WINE.

PREPARATION.—1st. Clean and wash the fish, dispose them on a buttered dish. 2d. and 3d. Do as 2d. and 3d. for the Truite au vin Blanc, No. 76.

SMELT.

124. EPERLANS FRITS.

FRIED SMELTS.

As for the Merlans Frits, No. 122.

HERRING.

125. HARENGS GRILLES SAUCE MOUTARDE.

BROILED HERRINGS WITH MUSTARD SAUCE

Herring............6.	Salt and pepper......To suit the taste.
Olive Oil..........2 tablespoonsful.	*Time.*—⅓ hour.

PREPARATION.—1st. Clean and wash the herring, notch the flancs (the notches should be 1½ inches apart and ⅛ inch deep, to thoroughly cook the inside as well as the outside); pour some olive oil over; sprinkle some salt and pepper; broil and serve with a sauce moutarde. (For the sauce see No. 157.)

COD.

126. CABILLAUD AU COURT BOUILLON.

BOILED COD.

126a Sauce Hollandaise.   126b Sauce aux Capres.

As for the Truite au Court Bouillon, No. 67.

For the sauces see Nos. 151 and 152.

127. MORUE.

SALT COD.

127a Au beurre fondu.   127b Sauce aux Capres.

PROPORTIONS.—For five persons:

Salted cod........ ....4 lbs.	Butter............. ....¼ lb.
	Time.—1 hour.

PREPARATION.—1st. Freshen the cod for 24 hours, taking care to change the water about 4 or 5 times.   2d. One hour before serving place this cod in a kettle with *cold* water, let boil, and as soon as it boils place the kettle on a corner of the range and allow to simmer for about ¾ hour.   3d. Place on a warm dish and serve with ⅛ lb. butter, placed on the fish and melted by the heat of the fish itself, or with a caper sauce apart.   Serve always boiled potatoes with the cod.

For Caper sauce see No. 152.

PERCH.

128. PERCHES FRITTES.

FRIED PERCH.

As Fried Whiting, No. 122.

129. SALADE DE FILLETS DE PERCHES.

PERCH SALAD.

PROPORTIONS.—For five persons:

Perch... ....10 lbs.	Oil............ ....6 tablespoonsful.
Hard eggs..... 3.	Vinegar ....3 tablespoonsful.
Lettuce salad..1 handful.	Salt and pepper...To suit the taste.
Parsley...........⅓ handful.	*Time.*—¾ hour.

PREPARATION.—1st. Clean and wash the perch, cut off the fins, remove the fillets, wash and let them drip. 2d. Have ready in a kettle enough boiling salted water, drop the fillets in, let boil a while, then place the kettle on a corner of the range and let it simmer for 5 minutes. 3d. Drip the fillets, and let them cool. 4th. When ready to serve dispose them in a salad dish with 1 handful lettuce salad, sliced quite fine, dispose over 3 hard eggs cut in 4, mix in a bowl 6 tablespoonsful oil, 3 tablespoonsful vinegar, salt and pepper according to the taste, 1 tablespoonful hashed parsley. Pour this seasoning over the perch and serve cold.

GUDGEONS.

130. FRITURE DE GOUGEONS.

FRIED GUDGEONS.

As for the Fried Whiting, No. 122.

STURGEON.

131. ESTURGEON A LA RUSSE.

STURGEON A LA RUSSE.

PROPORTIONS.—For five persons:

Sturgeon.........4 to 5 lbs.	Stock............... 1 glassful.
Vegetables......1 carrot, 1 onion, 12 small onions.	Vinegar............⅓ glassful. Mushrooms, sliced 2 tablespoonsful
Butter..... ....5 tablespoonsful.	Pickled gherkins, sliced, 2 table-
Flour...........2 tablespoonsful.	spoonfuls.
White wine .... 1 glassful.	*Time.*—¾ hour.

PREPARATION.—1st. Clean and wash 4 to 5 lb. steak of sturgeon, place it in a kettle with enough cold water to cover it well; add 1 onion and 1 carrot sliced fine; ¼ glassful vinegar; boil slowly for about ¼ hour. 2d. During that time prepare a sauce as follows: Melt in a sauce pan 2 tablespoonsful butter mixed with 2 tablespoonsful flour, then add 1 glassful white wine, 1 glassful stock, cook awhile, add the mushrooms, the gherkins, the small onions (previously cooked in some boiling water), let cook awhile and then add 3 tablespoonsful fresh butter.   4th. Place the sturgeon, cut in slices 1 inch thick on a dish and pour the sauce over

132. ESTURGEON FROID. SAUCE RAIFORD.

COLD STURGEON, HORSERADISH SAUCE.

1st. Cook the sturgeon as above, let it cool, cut it in slices and serve with horseradish sauce, No. 166.

LOBSTER.

133. HOMARD GRILLE

BROILED LOBSTER.

133a Sauce Mayonnaise.   133b Sauce Tartare.
133c Sauce Remoulade.

PROPORTIONS.

Lobster...2 of about 2 lbs. each.   Salt and pepper....To suit the taste.
Olive oil ....4 tablespoonsful.   Parsley.................⅛ handful.

PREPARATION.— 1st. Cut the lobster in two endwise, place those halves

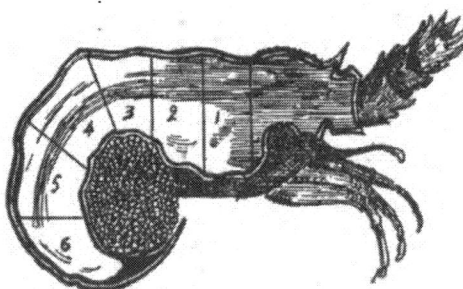

on a dish, pour over some salt and pepper, and about 4 tablespoonsful olive oil.   2d. Let broil on a light fire, for about ½ hour, taking care to turn them from time to time. 3d. Serve on a dish with green parsley around and the sauce apart, No. 162, 163, 164.

134. HOMARD FROID.

COLD BOILED LOBSTER.

134a Sauce Mayonnaise.   134b Sauce Tartare.
134c Sauce Remoulade.

HOW TO BUY A BOILED LOBSTER.—It is economical and time saving to buy ready cooked lobsters.   To be good they should

1st. Be without bad odor   2d. Be heavy.

3d. The tail should be folded under the body so firmly that you cannot easily unfold it.

HOW TO BOIL A LOBSTER.—1st. Choose a heavy live lobster, wash and brush it, tie the claws and the tail with some twine.   2d. Place the lobster in a kettle with boiling salted water, let boil awhile then put the kettle on a corner of the range and let simmer for about ⅓ hour. (2 lb. lobster. Dip and let cool.

For the sauces see No. 162, 163, 164.

135. HOMARD A L'AMERICAINE.

PROPORTIONS:

Lobster..........2 of 2 lbs. each.	White wine ....1 glassful.
Butter...........7 tablespoonsful.	Stock.....................1 glassful.
Brandy..........⅓ glassful.	Parsley. ....⅓ handful.

PREPARATION.—1st. Cut the tail in slices 1½ inches thick, and the bodies endwise and crosswise. 2d. Let warm in a stew pan (quite large) 3 tablespoonsful of butter; add the lobsters, some salt, white and red pepper; allow to cook for 5 to 6 minutes (till the lobsters become quite red). 3d. Add ⅓ glassful brandy; let boil till the brandy begins to burn; then add 1 glassful white wine, 1 glass stock; let boil on bright fire for five minutes, and when ready to serve add 4 tablespoonsful fresh butter mixed with some hashed parsley. *Don't let boil again;* and serve ·in a warm hollow dish.

136. SALADE DE HOMARD.

LOBSTER SALAD.

PROPORTIONS.—For five persons:

Cooked lobsters.....4 lbs.	Oil ....3 tablespoonsful.
Or, canned lobsters 2 lbs.	Vinegar............1 tablespoonful.
Lettuce ....2 pieces.	Mayonnaise sauce.1 pint.
Hard boiled eggs ..3.	Salt and pepper ...To suit the taste.
Green olives.........12.	

PREPARATION.—1st. Shell the lobsters (or let drip the canned lobsters); cut the flesh in slices, and let them pickle with salt, pepper, oil and vinegar for about 15 minutes. 2d. Clean the lettuces; dispose the leaves in a salad dish; place the lobster slices over; sprinkle 1 tablespoonful hashed parsley, and pour over 1 pint mayonnaise sauce (No. 162). 3d. To give a fine appearance to the dish, dispose gently over it 3 hard boiled eggs cut in 4, some lettuce leaves, 12 green olives, also some nice slices of lobster; let cool awhile in an ice-box and serve cold.

137. COTELETTES DE HOMARD.

Lobster Chops.

PROPORTIONS.—For five persons:

Lobsters........2 of 3 lbs. each.	Mushrooms............¼ lb. can.
Butter ....7 tablespoonsful.	Oysters..................12.
Flour ....2 tablespoonsful.	Truffles ....⅛ lb. can.
Madeira........1 glassful.	*Time.*—½ hour.

PREPARATION.—1st. Shell the tails and the claws of 2 cooked lobsters; cut about 10 steaks ½ inch thick; dispose them in crown on a buttered dish and insert in each of the slices one small paw to imitate the handle of a chop. 2d. Cut off all the parings of the chops and all the flesh you can take from the shell; slice ¼ lb. mushrooms (canned or previously cooked), also ⅛ can of truffles, 12 oysters cooked as indicated (No. 77). 3d. Place the chops in an oven to warm them. 4th. During that time let melt in a saucepan 2 tablespoonsful butter mixed with 2 tablespoonsful flour, the juice of the mushrooms, truffles, oysters, 1 glassful Madeira; let boil for awhile and add the chopped flesh, the mushrooms, oysters, truffles, etc.; let cook again for 5 minutes; place the saucepan on a corner of the range; add 3 yolks mixed with 3 tablespoonsful fresh butter; *don't allow to boil again*, and pour this garnish in the middle of the crown formed by the lobster's chops.

138. COQUILLES DE HOMARD A LA CALIFORNIENNE.

As for the Coquilles de Truite, No. 82, replacing the flesh of the fish by lobster flesh.

SHRIMP.

139. BUISSON DE CREVETTES.

Boiled Shrimps.

PROPORTIONS.—About ¼ lb. for each guest.

PREPARATION.—To boil shrimps, just dip them awhile in salted boiling water. Let drip and serve on a dish with green parsley.

CRAWFISH.

140. ECREVISSES EN BUISSON.

Boiled Crawfish.

PROPORTIONS.—For five persons:

Crawfish............................50.	Parsley ....2 handsful.
Onion............,........ ....1.	White wine.............½ pint.
Carrot................................1.	*Time.*—½ hour.

PREPARATION.—1st. Cook the crawfish alive in a sauce pan, with ⅓ pint white wine(or water with a little vinegar), one onion, one carrot sliced, till well red, taking care to turn them from time to time. 2d. Let them cool in their own juice, while turning from time to time. 3d. When cold let them drip and dispose gently on a dish with green parsley.

141. ECREVISSES BORDELAISE.

CRAWFISH A LA BORDELAISE.

PROPORTIONS.—For five persons:

Crawfish.........25.	Brandy..................⅛ glassful.
Onions ....- 2.	Hashed parsley......
Carrot........... 1.	Salt...................,.
Butter........... 5 tablespoonsful.	Pepper, white and red.
White wine......2 glassesful.	*Time.*—20 minutes.

PREPARATION.—1st. Cook in a sauce pan for 5 minutes 2 chopped onions and 1 carrot cut in small dices in 2 tablespoonsful butter, add 2 glassesful white wine and the crawfish, with salt, red and white pepper; let cook for 5 minutes, and when ready to serve add 1 glassful brandy, 3 tablespoonsful butter and some hashed parsley; serve in a hollow dish.

SOFT SHELL CRABS.

142. CRABES MOUS FRITS.

FRIED SOFT SHELL CRABS.

PROPORTIONS.—For five persons:

Soft shell crabs.............. 20.	Butter.........................¼ lb.
Bread crumbs.........5 tablespoonsful.	

PREPARATION.— After lifting up the shell, remove the spongy substance found on the back, wash and then drip them on a napkin. 2d. Dip them in beaten eggs, roll them in bread crumbs, fry slowly in butter until you obtain a yellow color. 3d. Serve on a folded napkin with fried parsley.

OYSTERS.

143. HUITERS FRAICHES.

OYSTERS ON THE HALF SHELL.

See No. 54.

144. HUITRES FRITTES.

FRIED OYSTERS.

PROPORTIONS.—For five persons:

Oysters......................5 doz.   Bread crumbs...4 tablespoonsful.
Eggs.........................3.   Butter.............¼ lb.

PREPARATION.—1st. Take the oysters from the shell, dip them in beaten eggs, roll in bread crumbs and fry in butter. 2d. Serve on a folded napkin.

145. HUITRES GRILLEES.

BROILED OYSTERS.

PROPORTIONS:

Oysters............................5 doz.   Butter.........5 tablespoonsful.
Bread crumbs....................4 tablespoonsful.

PREPARATION.—1st. Take the oysters from the shell, dip them in melted butter, roll in bread crumbs and broil on bright fire. 2d. Serve on a folded napkin.

146. HUITRES A LA POULETTE.

OYSTERS A LA POULETTE.

PROPORTIONS:

Oysters...........5 doz.   Lemons......................1.
Butter............4 tablespoonsful.   White wine.............⅓ pint.
Flour.............1 tablespoonful.   White pepper, a little...
Yolks.............2.   *Time.*—½ hour.

PREPARATION.—1st. Place the oysters in a sauce pan, let them boil in their own juice and ⅓ pint white wine, some white pepper but no salt; let them drip and put the juice apart. 2d. Melt in a sauce pan 2 tablespoonsful butter mixed with 1 tablespoonful flour, add while stirring the juice of the oysters through a napkin because it always contains some sand. 3d. When ready to serve, add 2 yolks, 2 tablespoonsful butter and the juice of a lemon. Don't allow to boil and serve in a hollow dish.

MUSSELS.

147. MOULES A LA MARINIERE.

MUSSELS A LA MARINIERE.

PROPORTIONS.—For five persons:

Mussels................2 quarts.   Butter.........................¼ lb.
Parsley ....½ handful.   *Time.*—¼ hour.

PREPARATION.—1st. Clean, brush and wash the mussels. 2d. Place them in a sauce pan with 2 tablespoonsful hashed parsley, very little salt, some white pepper. Let cook on a bright fire for about five minutes and serve with the shells in a hollow dish.

148. MOULES A LA POULETTE.

MUSSELS A LA POULETTE.

Mussels..........2 quarts.		Yolks........................2.	
Butter............¼ lb.		White wine...............⅓ pint.	
Flour ....1 tablespoonful.		White pepper ....A little.	
Lemon...........1.		*Time.*—¼ hour.	

PREPARATION.—1st and 2nd. Same as above but take off one shell on two, then do as indicated for the Oysters a la Poulette, No. 146.

FROGS.

149. GRENOUILLES FRITTES.

FRIED FROGS.

PROPORTIONS.—For five persons:

Frogs...........3 dozen.		Lemon ....1.	
Milk ....2 glassesful.		Butter......Enough to fry with.	
Flour............3 tablespoonsful.		*Time.*—⅓ hour.	

PREPARATION.—1st. Have ready skinned frogs or do as follows: Skin the frogs, keep only the hind legs and the quarters, and let them stand in fresh water for one hour to whiten the flesh. 2d. Dip them in milk, roll in flour and then fry in butter until well colored. Serve with a lemon cut in four.

150. GRENOUILLÈS A LA POULETTE.

FROGS A LA POULETTE.

PROPORTIONS.—For five persons:

Frogs............3 dozen.		Stock ....⅓ glassful.	
Butter..........⅓ lb.		Yolks....................2.	
Flour ....2 tablespoonsful.		Parsley................⅓ handful.	
White wine...1 glassful.		*Time.*—¼ hour.	

PREPARATION.—1st. Do as 1st. No. 149. 2d. Stew in 3 tablespoonsful butter, 1 glassful white wine, ⅓ glassful stock; boil on a bright fire for 5 minutes, add ¼ lb. butter mixed with two tablespoonsful flour, and when ready to serve add 2 yolks, the juice of a lemon and 1 tablespoonful hashed parsley.

SAUCES TO BE SERVED WITH FISH.

1. Warm Sauces.

151. SAUCES HOLLANDAISE.*

HOLLANDAISE SAUCE. (*White.*)

PROPORTIONS.—For five persons:

Butter	¾ lb.	Salt and white pepper	...To suit the taste.
Yolks	3.		
Flour	2 tablespoonsful.	Water	1 glassful.
Lemon	1.	*Time.*—10 minutes.	

PREPARATION.—1st. Place in a sauce pan (on a corner of the range or, better, in another sauce pan half full of boiling water) ¼ lb. butter mixed with 2 tablespoonsful flour (use a wooden spoon), add the juice of 1 lemon, a little salt and white pepper (also rasped nutmeg if liked), 1 glassful water; stir well the whole till the pap becomes uniform. 2d. Add while stirring 3 yolks, then in small pieces about ½ lb. butter (very fresh), always stirring and never allowing to boil. Serve this sauce apart.

152. SAUCE AUX CAPRES.

CAPER SAUCE. (*White.*)

As for the Hollandaise Sauce, No. 151, but when ready to serve add 2 tablespoonsful pickled capers.

153. SAUCE AUX HUITRES.

OYSTER SAUCE. (*White.*)

PROPORTIONS.—For five persons:

Oysters	3 doz.	Stock	½ glassful.
Butter	½ lb.	Starch	1 tablespoonful.
Yolks	3.	Salt and white pepper	...To suit the taste.
White wine	1 glassful.		
		Time.—20 minutes.	

PREPARATION.—1st. Cook in a sauce pan 3 dozen oysters, in their own juice and also 1 glassful white wine, ½ glassful stock, a little salt and white pepper (also rasped nutmeg if liked). 2d. After boiling one minute drip the oysters, place them in a sauce bowl, and pour the juice in another sauce pan through a sifter or a napkin (there being always some sand, etc., in the oyster's juice). 3d. Warm this juice again and add while stirring 3 yolks and ½ lb. butter; don't allow to boil again and pour into the sauce bowl over the oysters.

---

* This is a simplified recipe for family use, but is quite as palatable as the complicated ones, which require some practice and are quite expensive.

154. SAUCE CARDINAL.

(Rose.)

PROPORTIONS.—For five persons:

Lobster.. ....1 of about 2 lbs.	Flour.................2 tablespoonsful.
Butter...... ....¼ lb.	Yolks...................2.
Fish stock.......2 glassesful.	Carmine..............A little bit.

Time.—¼ hour.

PREPARATION.—1st. Melt in a sauce pan ¼ lb. butter mixed with 2 tablespoonsful flour, stir well the whole with a wooden spoon. 2d. Add 2 glassesful of fish stock (No. 69) let boil a while, then place the sauce pan on a corner of the range and while stirring add the 2 yolks, the juice of a lemon, a little bit carmine to give the color and little by little about ¼ lb. butter. 2d. Slice the flesh of a lobster, dispose the slices on and around the fish and pour the sauce over.

155. SAUCE CREVETTE.

SHRIMP SAUCE. *(Rose.)*

156. SAUCE HOMARD.

LOBSTER SAUCE. *(Rose.)*

PREPARATION.—Make a Hollandaise Sauce (No. 151) add a very little carmine to give color and about ¼ lb. shrimp tails for the first and ¼ lb. of lobster sliced for the second.

157. SAUCE MOUTARDE.

MUSTARD SAUCE. *(Yellow.)*

PROPORTIONS.—For five persons:

Mustard.........2 tablespoonsful.	Water..................1 glassful.
Butter............2 tablespoonsful.	Salt and pepper....To suit the taste.
Flour............1 tablespoonsful.	Parsley...............⅓ handful.

Time.—¼ hour.

PREPARATION.—Melt in a sauce pan 2 tablespoonsful butter mixed with 1 tablespoonful flour, add while stirring about 1 glassful warm water, 2 tablespoonsful mustard, some salt and pepper and let boil awhile till quite thick. Serve this sauce apart.

158. SAUCE GENEVOISE.

GENEVESE SAUCE. *(Red.)*

PROPORTIONS.—For five persons:

Onion....................1	Flour ....2 tablespoonsful.
Parsley ....⅓ handful.	Red wine.. ....1 glassful.
Thyme and laurel...A little.	Anchovies.. ....2 (pickled.)
Butter ....¼ lb.	*Time.*—¾ hour.

PREPARATION.—1st. Let brown one onion chopped with one table-spoonful butter, sprinkle over 2 tablespoonsful flour, add 1 glassful red wine, some thyme and laurel, ⅓ handful parsley, let cook slowly for about ¼ hour. 2d. Pass the whole through a sifter, pour the pap obtained in another sauce pan, add little by little about ¼ lb butter and 2 anchovies broken fine in some of the butter. Don't allow to boil again and serve apart.

159. SAUCE POLONAISE.

POLISH SAUCE. (*Yellow.*)

PROPORTIONS.—For five persons:

Butter	¾ lb.	Parsley	⅛ handful.
Hard eggs	Three.	*Time.*—10 minutes.	

PREPARATION.—Let the butter melt; add the eggs and the parsley, both chopped fine; stir well the whole and serve in a sauce bowl apart.

160. SAUCE PROVENCALE.

TOMATO SAUCE A LA PROVENÇALE. (*Red.*)

PROPORTIONS.—For five persons:

Onion	One.	Tomato sauce	3 tablespoonsful.
Garlic clove	One.	Parsley	¼ handful.
Butter	4 tablespoonsful.	*Time.*—	

PREPARATION.—Chop the onion and garlic; let them brown with 1 tablespoonful butter; add 3 tablespoonsful tomato catsup, 2 tablespoonsful butter and hashed parsley. 2d. Stir well the whole and pour over the fish.

161. MAITRE D'HOTEL.

MELTED BUTTER WITH CHOPPED PARSLEY. (*Yellow.*)

We call a *maitre d'hotel* some fresh butter mixed with chopped parsley, which you place not *melted* over some fish or meat. It should be melted by the heat of the dish.

162. SAUCE MAYONNAISE.

MAYONNAISE SAUCE. (*Yellow.*)

PROPORTIONS.—For five persons:

Yolks	Two.	Vinegar	1 tablespoonful.
Oil	⅛ pint.	Salt and pepper	A little.
		Time.—¼ hour.	

PREPARATION.—1st. Place in a bowl 2 yolks, which you beat well with some salt and white pepper; then add, *drop by drop*, and while stirring, about ⅙ pint olive oil. 2d. The pap being quite thick, add, little by little and while stirring, about 1 tablespoonful good vinegar (of white wine or cider). 3d. Continue to stir and add as indicated above the remainder of your oil.

NOTE.—This sauce should be made in a cold place, and will require some practice.

163. SAUCE TARTARE.

TARTARE SAUCE. (*Yellow.*)

Same as for the above (No. 162), but when ready to serve add about 2 tablespoonsful chopped green onion and gherkins.

164. SAUCE REMOULADE.

(*Light Brown.*)

PROPORTIONS.—For five persons:

Mustard (powder)..1 tablespoonful. Parsley }
Water..................1 glassful. Ciboul } ...¼ handful of each.
Oil......................1 glassful. Green onion }
Vinegar ....⅛ glassful. *Time.*—10 minutes.

PREPARATION.—Stir in a bowl 1 tablespoonful mustard with 1 glassful water. 2d. Add, little by little, 1 glassful oil and ⅛ glassful vinegar. 3d. When ready to serve, add the chopped parsley, green onion, ciboul, etc.

165. SAUCE VINAIGRETTE.

VINEGAR SAUCE. (*Green.*)

PROPORTIONS.—For five persons:

Vinegar...........1 glassful. Parsley.............¼ handful.
Olive oil ....1 glassful. Ciboul..............¼ handful.
Pickled gherkins.....Twelve.

PREPARATION.—Chop the parsley and ciboul; cut the gherkins in small dices; put in a bowl with 1 glassful olive oil, 1 glassful vinegar; salt and pepper to suit the taste and mix well together.

166. SAUCE RAIFORT.

HORSERADISH SAUCE. (*White.*)

PROPORTIONS.—For five persons:

Horseradish ....2 or 3 stalks. Vinegar..................1 glassful.
Salt and pepper to suit the taste.

PREPARATION.—1st. Grate the horseradish; put the pap in a bowl with some salt and white pepper, and pour over 1 glassful vinegar.

RECAPITULATION.

SALMON OR TROUT.

67. Saumon or Truite au Court Bouillon...........Boiled Salmon or Trout.
        67a Sauce Hollandaise.   } Hollandaise Sauce.
        67b Sauce aux Capres..............with } Caper Sauce.
        67c Sauce Polonaise.   } Polish Sauce.

68. Saumon or Truite au Bleu.
            Sauce Genevoise.

69. Saumon or Truite au Blanc.
        69a Sauce aux huitres.....................With oysters.
        69b Sauce cardinal.............................
        69c Sauce homard.............................Lobster sauce.
        69d Sauce crevette.............................Shrimp sauce.

70. Truite au vin Blance.............................With white wine.
71. Truite au Gratin...
72. Saumon Grillè.......................................Broiled salmon.
        72a Maitre d'hotel.
        72b Sauce Mayonnaise.
        72c Sauce Tartare.
        72d Sauce Remoulade.
        72e Sauce Vinaigrette.

73. Petites Truites a la Meuniere.....................Brook trouts.
74. Fillets de Truite Frits a la Colbert................ } Fried fillets of trout
                                      a la Colbert.
75. Fillets de Truite au Gratin...........................
76.   "   "   " au vin Blanc......................With white wine.
77.   "   "   " Normande.........................
78.   "   "   " a la Creme........................With cream.
79.   "   "   " a la Tanty........................

80. Saumon Froid
        or   } A l'Imperiale.
    Truite Froide

81. Saumon Froid or Truite Froide.
        81a Sauce Mayonnaise.
        81b Sauce Tartare.
        81c Sauce Remoulade.
        81d Sauce Vinaigrette.

82. Coquilles de Saumon
        or   } A la Californienne.
   Coquilles de Truite.

PIKE.

83. Pike au Court Bouillon.
        83a Sauce Hollandaise.
        83b Sauce aux capres.
        83c Sauce Polonaise.

84. Pike au Bleu.
        Sauce Genevoise.

85. Pike au Blanc.
        85a Sauce aux huitres.
        85b Sauce cardinal.
        85c Sauce homard.
        85d Sauce crevette.
86. Pike au vin Blanc.
87. Pike au Gratin.
88. Fillets de Pike Frits a la Colbert.
89. Fillet de Pike au Gratin.
90.   "   "   au Vin Blanc.
91.   "   "   Normande.
92.   "   "   a la Creme.
93.   "   "   a la Tanty.
94. Pike Froid a l'Imperiale.
95. Pike Froid.
        95a Sauce Mayonnaise.
        95b Sauce Tartare.
        95c Sauce Remoulade.
        95d Sauce Vinaigrette.
96. Coquilles de Pike a la Californienne

PICKEREL.

97. Brochet au Bleu.
      Sauce Genevoise.
98. Brochet a la Juive.
99. Brochet Froid.
        99a Sauce Mayonnaise.
        99b Sauce Tartare.
        99c Sauce Remoulade.
        99d Sauce Vinaigrette.

CARP.

100. Carpe au Bleu.
      Sauce Genevoise.
101. Carpe a la Juive.
102. Carpe Frite.
103. Carpes en Matelotte.

EEL.

104. Anguille Grillee Sauce Tartare.
105. Anguille en Matelotte.
106. Matelotte a la Mariniére.

BLACK BASS.

107. Black Bass aux Fines Herbes.
108. Black Bass Grillé.
        108a Maitre d'hotel.
        108b Sauce Mayonnaise.
        108c Sauce Tartare.
        108d Sauce Remoulade.
109. Black Bass Frit.

SHAD.

110. Alose Grillee.
- 110a Maitre d'hotel.
- 110b Sauce Mayonnaise.
- 110c Sauce Tartare.
- 110d Sauce Remoulade.

111. Oeufs d Alose Grillés Maitre d'hotel.

RED SNAPPER.

112. Red Snapper Grillé.
- 112a Maitre d'hotel.
- 112b Sauce Mayonnaise.
- 112c Sauce Tartare.
- 112d Sauce Remoulade.
- 112e Sauce Provencale.

WHITE FISH.

113. White Fish Grillè.
- 113a Maitre d'hotel.
- 113b Sauce Mayennaise.
- 113c Sauce Tartare.
- 113d Sauce Remoulade.

SOLE.

114. Sole Fritte.
115. Fillets de Solle Frits a la Colbert.
116. Fillets de Solle au Gratin.
117.   "   "   " au vin Blanc.
118.   "   "   " Normande.
119.   "   "   " a la Creme.
120.   "   "   " a la Tanty.

MACKEREL.

121. Maquerau Grille.

Maitre d'hotel.

WHITING.

122. Merlans Frits.
123. Merlans au vin Blanc.

SMELTS.

124. Eperlans Frits.

HERRING.

125. Hareng Grille
- 125a Maitre d'hotel.
- 125b Sauce Moutarde.

COD.

126. Cabillaud au Court Bouillon.
- 126a Sauce Hollandaise.
- 126b Sauce aux Capres.

127. Morue.
- 127a Au Beurre Londu.
- 127b Sauce aux Capres.

PERCH.

128. Perches Frittes.
129. Salade de Fillets de Perches.

GUDGEONS.

130. Friture de Gougeons.

STURGEON.

131. Esturgeon a la Russe.
132. Esturgeon Froid.

Sauce Raifort.

LOBSTER.

133. and 134.   Homard Grille.

Homard Froid.
133a-134a   Sauce Mayonnaise.
133b-134b   Sauce Tartare.
133c-134c   Sauce Remoulade.

135. Homard a l'Americaine.
136. Salade de Homard.
137. Cotelettes de Homard.
138. Coquilles de Homard.

SHRIMP.

139. Buisson de Crevettes.

CRAWFISH.

140. Buisson d'Ecrevisses.
141. Ecrevisses a la Bordelaise.

SOFT SHELL CRABS.

142. Crabs Mous Frits a l'Americaine.

OYSTER.

143. Huitres Fraiches.
144. Huitres Frittes.
145. Huitres Grillees.
146. Huitres a la Poulette.

MUSSELS.

147. Moules a la Mariniere.
148. Moules a la Poulette.

FROGS.

149. Grenouilles Frittes.
150. Grenouilles a la Poulette.

FISH SOUPS.

SEE THE SOUPS.

SAUCES TO BE SERVED WITH FISH.

WARM SAUCES.	151.	Sauce Hollandaise.........White.
	152.	Sauce aux Capres.........Caper sauce, white.
	153.	Sauce aux Huîtres........Oyster sauce, white.
	154.	Sauce Cardinal............Rose.
	155.	Sauce Crevette.............Shrimp sauce, rose.
	156.	Sauce Homard............ Lobster sauce, rose.
	157.	Sauce Moutarde..........Mustard sauce, yellow.
	158.	Sauce Genevoise...........Genevese sauce, red.
	159.	Sauce Polonaise...........Polish sauce, yellow.
	160.	Sauce Provencale.........Tomato sauce, red.
	161.	Maitre d'hotel.............Melted Butter, yellow.
COLD SAUCES.	162.	Sauce Mayonnaise.......Mayonnaise sauce, light yellow.
	163.	Sauce Tartare.............Tartare sauce.
	164.	Sauce Remoulade........Light brown.
	165.	Sauce Vinaigrette........
	166.	Sauce Raifort.............Horseradish sauce.

EGGS.

Although eggs are ordinarily served for breakfast or lunch, Omelet with preserved fruit, No. 190; Omelet with rum, No. 191; Snow Eggs, No. 192, etc., etc., constitute very palatable sweet dishes for dinners.

167. OEUFS A LA COQUE.

SOFT BOILED EGGS.

PROPORTIONS.

Eggs (very fresh)...2 to 3 for each guest.
Time.—2 to 2½ minutes.

PREPARATION.—1st. Assure yourself by knocking gently one egg against another that there are no cracks in the shells; you will easily recognize that by the sound. 2d. Wash the eggs in cold water and if dirty, clean them by rubbing with some salt. 3d. Cook in boiling water for 2 to 2½ minutes, and serve in egg cups.

168. OEUFS DURS.

HARD BOILED EGGS.

PREPARATION.—1st and 2d as above. 3d. Cook the eggs for 10 minutes in boiling water, then dip them in cold water; by so doing they will be very easy to shell.

169. OEUFS A LA CREME.

EGGS WITH CREAM.

PROPORTIONS—For five persons:

Hard boiled eggs.....	10.	Butter.............1 tablespoonful.	
Onion...................	1.	Flour...............2 tablespoonsful.	
Milk	1 pint.	Parsley	

Time.—½ hour.

PREPARATION.—1st. Prepare the eggs as indicated in No. 168, shell them carefully, slice or cut them in four (4); place them in a sauce pan. 2d. In another sauce pan brown (light) 1 chopped onion, sprinkle over 2 tablespoonsful flour, add 1 pint milk and allow to cook while stirring for about 5 minutes. 3d. Pour this cream over the eggs, warm the whole without allowing to boil, and when ready to serve, sprinkle over some hashed parsley, and serve in a hollow dish.

170. SALADE D'OEUFS.

SALAD OF EGGS.

PROPORTIONS.

Hard boiled eggs.	10.	Salt and pepper...To suit the taste.	
Oil...............	4 tablespoonsful.	Parsley.	
Vinegar.........	3 tablespoonsful.	*Time.*—20 minutes.	

PREPARATION.—1st. Shell and slice the eggs, place them in a salad dish and pour over 4 tablespoonsful oil mixed with 3 tablespoonsful vinegar, salt and pepper (to suit the taste) and some hashed parsley.

171. OEUFS POCHES A LA PARISIENNE.

POACHED EGGS A LA PARISIENNE.

PROPORTIONS.—For five persons:

Eggs.........................10.		Truffles..............If liked.	
Ham........................ 4 oz.		Butter.. ....4 tablespoonsful.	
Mushrooms .... 6.		Flour.................1 tablespoonful.	
Tomato........ .... 1.		Madeira.. ....1 glassful.	
Fillets of fowl.............If liked.		Stock.................½ glassful.	

Time.—¼ hour.

PREPARATION.—1st. Poach the eggs as indicated in Note of No. 9, peel and place them in a hollow dish. 2d. Cut the ham in dices, slice the mushrooms, chop the tomato also (if you have some) cut in dices a cold fillet of fowl and place it together with 1 or 2 sliced truffles, in a sauce pan with two tablespoonsful butter and cook the whole for about 2 minutes; then sprinkle over 1 tablespoonful flour, add 1 glassful madeira and ¼ glassful stock, and stew for 2 minutes. 3d. Add 2 tablespoonsful butter, stir well the whole and pour over the eggs.

172. OEUFS A LA CHRISTOHPE COLOMB.

PROPORTIONS.—For five persons:

Poached eggs..................6.   Jelly of meat............ ....¼ lb.
Toasts ....6.   Butter...................................
Pate de foie gras.............¼ lb.   *Time.* — ½ hour.

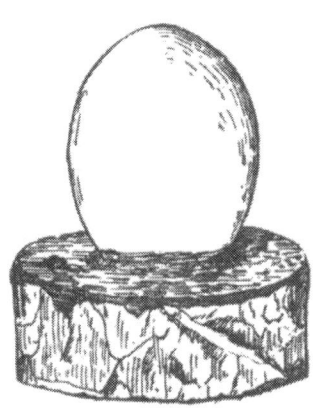

PREPARATION.—1st. Make small toast about 2½ inches in diameter and 1 inch thick, fry them in butter, lay over a coat of "Pate de Foie Gras" about ¼ inch thick, taking care to leave a hole in the middle. 2d. Dispose them on a warm dish and place upright on each toast in the hole menaged in the "Pate de Foie Grass" an egg poached as indicated No. 9 and carefully shelled. 3d. Let melt in a sauce pan ¼ lb. of "Jelly of Meat" and ¼ fresh butter, mix well the whole, don't allow to boil and pour over the eggs.

173. OEUFS A LA TZARINE.

EGGS A LA TZARINE.

PROPORTIONS.—For five persons:

Bread........................5 pieces.   Butter........... ....3 tablespoonsful.
Eggs............ ....5.   Salt and pepper....A little.
                    Time.—½ hour.

PREPARATION.—1st. Cut 5 pieces of bread about 3 inches in diameter and 3 inches in height. Cut the crust off and make in the middle of each a hole about 1½ inches in diameter and 2 inches deep, fry these toasts in butter. 2d. Dispose them in a buttered dish, break a fresh egg in every hole, sprinkle over some salt and pepper, place about 1 teaspoonful butter on each egg, and let them bake for 5 minutes.

NOTE. This dish, notwithstanding its simplicity, may be served for the most fashionable breakfasts or lunches and was highly appreciated by the late Tzarine.

174. OEUFS FRITS.

FRIED EGGS.

PROPORTIONS.—For one person:

Eggs...................................2   Olive oil.............2 tablespoonsful.
                    Time.—10 minutes.

NOTE. The eggs should be fried one at a time.

---

* Eggs should be fried just at the moment of serving and be very warm to be palatable; therefore we do not recommend them when there are more than 4 or 5 persons.

PREPARATION.—1st. Warm the oil in a small frying pan and when very hot incline the pan a little, break the egg in the oil and let fry for about 3 minutes taking care in turning to fry both sides and not break it. 2d. Let drip and serve on a folded napkin.

175. OEUFS SUR LE PLAT.

SHIRRED EGGS.

PROPORTIONS.—For one person:

Eggs..............2 to 3.   Salt and pepper...To suit the taste.
Butter. ....1 tablespoonful.   *Time.*—10 minutes.

PREPARATION No. 1.—Have as many small dishes as you have guests, butter them, break the eggs in a sauce pan, one at a time*, slip them into the dish, sprinkle over some salt and pepper and allow to cook for 5 minutes in an oven.

No. 2.—1st. Break the eggs in a sauce pan, one at a time* and slip them into a frying pan, where you have melted the butter in advance. 2d. Cook for about 5 minutes and slip the eggs into a warm dish or plate.

NOTE.—The former way is more fashionable.

176. OEUFS AU JAMBON.

HAM AND EGGS.

PROPORTIONS.—For one person:

Eggs......................2 to 3.   Butter ....1 tablespoonful.
Ham......................2 oz.   Salt and pepper...To suit the taste.
Time.—10 minutes.

PREPARATION.—1st. Slice the ham and place the slices on the buttered dish, then do as indicated above in No. 175.

177. OEUFS AU LARD.

EGGS WITH BACON.

PROPORTIONS AND PREPARATION.—As for the above, but use bacon (not too fat) instead of ham.

178. OEUFS BROUILLES AUX CROUTONS.

SCRAMBLED EGGS WITH TOAST.

PROPORTIONS.—For five persons:

Eggs......................10.   Salt and pepper...To suit the taste.
Butter....................¼ lb.   *Time.*—10 minutes.

* By doing this you will recognize a bad egg, and it will not spoil the others.

PREPARATION.—1st. Break the eggs (as in No. 175), slip them into a sauce pan where you beat them with ¼ lb. butter, salt and pepper to suit the taste (also some rasped nutmeg if liked). *All this should be done before placing the sauce pan on the fire.* 2d. Allow to cook while stirring for about 5 minutes on a light fire and when the pap becomes quite thick, pour the whole into a hollow dish and serve with fried toasts on and around the eggs.

179. OEUFS BROUILLES AUX FROMAGE.

SCRAMBLED EGGS WITH CHEESE.

As for the above, but add ¼ lb. rasped cheese (Parmesan or Swiss), while mixing the eggs with the butter.

180. OEUFS BROUILLES AUX POINTES D'ASPERGE.

SCRAMBLED EGGS WITH ASPARAGUS TOPS.

PROPORTIONS.—For five persons:

Eggs...........................8.	Asparagus ....2 bunches.
Butter ....¼ lb.	Salt and pepper.. To suit the taste.

Time.—¼ hour.

PREPARATION.—1st. Take the tender part of the asparagus (green ones preferred) and cut them in pieces about ½ inch long, cook them in some salted water for about 10 minutes and let them drip. 2d. Do as indicated in 1st. and 2d., No. 178, and when the eggs are quite cooked add the asparagus tops, mix well the whole with a wooden spoon and serve in a hollow dish with toast.

181. OEUFS BROUILLES AUX QUEUES D'ECREVISSE.

SCRAMBLED EGGS WITH CRAWFISH TAILS.

182. OEUFS BROUILLES A L'EMINCE DE HOMARD.

SCRAMBLED EGGS WITH MINCED LOBSTERS.

As for No. 180, but replace the asparagus by crawfish tails (cooked) or by lobster's flesh (also cooked), cut in small dices.

183. GENERAL REMARKS ON OMELETS.

In making an omelet care should be taken that the pan be clean, smooth and hot, otherwise the omelet will stick. To those who have not much practice in making omelets we recommend making several small omelets rather than a large one, for instance, for 5 persons make two omelets of 5 eggs each, instead of one of 10.

Allow 2 eggs for each guest and 1 tablespoonful milk; this makes the omelet more tender and puffy, but many prefer it without milk.

184. OMELETTE AUX FINES HERBES.

PLAIN OMELET WITH HASHED PARSLEY.

PROPORTIONS.——For five persons:

Eggs.................10.   Salt and pepper...To suit the taste.
Milk .... 1 glassful.   Parsley .... ⅛ handful.
Butter................ ¼ lb.   *Time.*—10 minutes.

PREPARATION.—1st. Break the eggs as indicated in No. 175, slip them into a salad-dish, beat well together with some salt, pepper and hashed parsley (also milk if used). 2d. Melt ¼ lb. butter in a frying pan on a bright fire and when the butter is well hot, pour the eggs in and stir well the whole with a *fork* till the pap becomes quite thick. 3d. Take the handle with the right hand, incline the pan while shaking so as to bring the omelet near one of the edges and begin to fold it. 4th. Turn the pan over a warm dish so as to fold the omelet in two.

Don't forget that a good omelet should be long, thick in the middle and soft inside.

185. OMELETTE AU FROMAGE.

CHEESE OMELET.

As the above, but instead of hashed parsley mix ¼ lb. rasped cheese (Swiss or Parmesan) with the eggs.

186. OMELETTE AU JAMBON.

HAM OMELET.

PROPORTIONS.—For five persons:
As for No. 184 and ¼ lb. cooked ham.
PRÉPARATION.—1st. Cut the ham in dices, let them fry a little in some butter. 2d. Do as indicated, No. 184, for plain omelet.

187. OMELETTE AU LARD.

OMELET WITH BACON.

PROPORTIONS.—For five persons:
As for No. 184 and ¼ lb. bacon.
PRÉPARATION.—1st. Cut the bacon in dices, allow them to cook awhile in some boiling water to freshen and soften them, and let them drip. 2d. Let them fry awhile in a frying pan, take the melted lard off, replace it by butter and do as indicated for the plain omelet, No. 184.

188. OMELETTE AUX ROGNONS.

OMELET WITH KIDNEYS.

PROPORTIONS.—For five persons:

As for No. 184.

Mutton kidneys..4 to 5.	Vinegar...........⅛ tablespoonful.
Butter..............1 tablespoonful.	Stock ....⅓ glassful.
Flour................1 tablespoonful.	Parsley.. ....A little.

Time.—20 minutes.

PREPARATION.—1st. Skin and slice the kidneys, let them cook awhile in a sauce pan with 1 tablespoonful butter, a little salt and pepper; sprinkle over 1 tablespoonful flour, add ⅛ tablespoonful vinegar, ⅓ glassful stock, some hashed parsley, let cook for 1 or 2 minutes and place the sauce pan on a corner of the range   2d. Make a plain omelet as indicated in No. 184, and at the time of turning it pour the kidneys in the gap formed in the middle of the omelet.

189. OMELETTE CELESTINE.

OMELET WITH CRAWFISH OR LOBSTERS.

PROPORTIONS.—For five persons:

As for No. 184.

Lobster......... ... . 2 lbs.	Milk ....1 glassful.
or Crawfish ....12.	Butter............1 tablespoonful.
Onion .... 1.	Flour ....1 tablespoonful.

Time.—½ hour.

PREPARATION.—1st. Shell the crawfish or the lobster, take the tails and the flesh of the claws in the former or cut the flesh in dices in the last case.   2d. Chop fine 1 small onion, let it brown in butter, add the crawfish or lobster flesh, some salt and pepper, sprinkle over 1 tablespoonful flour and add 1 glassful milk; boil awhile and place on the corner of the range.   3d. As 2d. in No. 188.

190. OMELETTE AUX CONFITURES.

OMELET WITH PRESERVED FRUITS.

PROPORTIONS.—For five persons:

As for No. 184 and

Preserved fruits.............½ lb.   Sugar..........3 tablespoonsful.

PREPARATION.—1st. Do as for the "Omelet with Kidneys." (No. 188.) Make a plain omelet, but replace the salt and pepper by 1 tablespoonful sugar and when about to turn the omelet pour ½ lb. preserved fruits in the gap formed in the middle of the omelet (See No. 184, 3d).   2d. When the omelet is on the dish, sprinkle 2 tablespoonsful granulated sugar over and burn this sugar, from place to place, with a red hot poker.

191. OMELETTE AU RHUM.

OMELET WITH RUM.

PROPORTIONS.—For five persons:

As for the above.

Rum..........................1 glassful.   *Time.*—20 minutes.

PREPARATION.—Do as for the above and when on the dish sprinkle some sugar over the omelet, pour over 1 glassful rum, light the rum and let it burn for about five minutes, while basting the omelet with a spoon.

CAUTION.—Never carry an omelet while burning but light it at the table.

192. OEUFS A LA NEIGE.

SNOW EGGS.

PROPORTIONS.—For five persons:

Eggs...............10.   Vanilla.........⎫
Sugar. ....8 tablespoonsful.   or Lemon Zest.. ⎬ ....A little.
Milk ....1 quart.   *Time.*—½ hour.

PREPARATION.—Break the eggs as indicated in No. 175, but slip the yolks in a sauce pan and beat the whites apart.   2d. Poach the whites, spoonful after spoonful, in boiling milk (1 quart milk, with 4 tablespoonsful sugar, a little vanilla or the zest of a lemon), boiling quickly in a somewhat flat sauce pan).   3d. Let them drip, and dispose in a hollow dish.   4th. Mix the yolks with 4 tablespoonsful sugar and pour into the sauce pan while stirring the warm milk where you have poached the eggs.   5th. Pour this sauce over the white and cool the whole in an icebox.   Serve cold.

RECAPITULATION.

I. SIDE DISHES FOR BREAKFAST OR LUNCH.

167. Oeufs a la Coque....................Soft boiled eggs.
168. Oeufs Durs ....Hard boiled eggs.
169. Oeufs a la Creme ....Hard boiled eggs with cream.
170. Salad D'Oeufs,......................Egg salad.
171. Oeufs Poches a la Parisienne...Poached eggs a la parisienne.
172 Oeufs a la Christophe Colomb.Eggs a la Christophe Colomb.
173. Oeufs a la Tzarine..................Eggs a la Tzarine.
174. Oeufs Frits.....,......................Fried eggs.
175. Oeufs sur le Plat....................Shirred eggs.
176. Oeufs au Jambon...................Ham and eggs.
177. Oeufs au Lard........ ....Bacon and eggs.
178. Oeufs Brouilles aux Croutons..Scrambled eggs with toast.
179. Oeufs Brouilles au Fromage...Scrambled eggs with cheese.
180. Oeufs Brouilles aux Pointes D'Asperge.....................} Scrambled eggs with asparagus tops.
181. Oeufs Brouilles aux Queues D'Ecrévisses ....} Scrambled eggs with crawfish tails.
182. Oeufs Brouilles a l'Emince de Homard....................} Scrambled eggs with lobster.
183. General Remark on Omelets.
184. Omelette au Fines Herbes......Plain omelet with parsley.
185. Omelette au Fromage....... ....Cheese omelet.
186. Omelette au Jambon........ .....Ham omelet.
187. Omelette au Lard ....Bacon omelet.
188. Omelette aux Rognons...........Kidney omelet.
189. Omelette Celestine ....Crawfish or lobster omelet.

II. SWEET DISHES FOR DINNERS.

190. Omelette aux Confitures........Omelet with preserved fruits.
191. Omelette aux Rhum..............Omelet with rum.
192. Oeufs a la Neige....................Snow eggs.

THE MEATS.

In a dinner the meats are certainly the most important parts; therefore it is natural that the cooks have done their utmost to present this most nourishing food under a good many forms.

Usually the meats are divided into "Releves, Entrees and Roasts." The former are quite large pieces of meat roasted or baked, but always served *entire* with sauce and garnishes. They are presented after the fish and appear chiefly at a great dinner. The second are meats *carved before being cooked*, broiled, roasted, baked, boiled or stewed, but always served with a sauce and some vegetable as a garnish. They are essentially family dishes, but are also served at every dinner as fashionable, it may be (lean dinner excepted, of course), and are served after the releve, if any. The last are *whole* roasted pieces, served with a salad after the entree and side dishes (vegetables*) and before sweet dishes.

---

*In some dinners the side dishes are served after the roast, but we recommend the former manner, especially when a salad is served with the roast—what should be always the case, provided there is a guest at your table.

BEEF.

193. ROSBIF A L'ANGLAISE.

ROAST BEEF*. (*Releve or Roast.*)

PROPORTIONS.—For a fine roast beef which may be served cold afterwards.

Beef (loin or fore ribs)....12 to 15 lbs.   Water or stock....1 glassful.
Water.........................1 glassful.   Salt..................To suit the taste.
Time.—1 hour to 1½ hours.

PREPARATION.—*To roast the beef.* 1st. Place the beef in an oblong stove pan (tinned or enameled); sprinkle some salt over; add one glass water and bake in a warm† oven from 1 hour to 1½ hours‡, while basting frequently.

Gravy.—The best sauce to be served with the roast beef is its own gravy, which you make as follows: When you have taken the roast beef from the pan, add one glass stock or water; let boil for one or two minutes on the range or stove; while stirring, skim the floating grease off, and pass this gravy through a fine strainer.

Garnishes.—When the roast beef is served as a releve, it should be accompanied by some vegetable as garnishes, especially with potatoes fried in butter, potato croquettes, stuffed tomatoes, etc. If served as a roast, it should be accompanied by salad.

194. COTE DE BOEUF NIVERNAISE.

FORE RIBS A LA NIVERNAISE. (*Releve.*)

PROPORTIONS AND PREPARATION.—Same as for the roast beef No. 193. Served with Carrots a la Nivernaise (No. 328) apart.

195. FILLET ROTI.

ROAST TENDERLOIN. (*Roast.*)

PROPORTIONS AND PREPARATION.—Same as for the Roast Beef No. 193, but roast only for about one hour.

---

*The best parts of beef for roasting are the loin and fore ribs. The middle ribs and shunk ribs may be employed, but are less tender.

†If the oven is not warm enough the meat will bake, but not roast.

‡You can be certain that the roast is well cooked by pressing it with your finger. If ready it is firm, and if not it is soft.

196. FILLET BRAISE JARDINIERE.

BRAISED TENDERLOIN JARDINIERE. (*Releve.*)

PROPORTIONS.—For ten persons:

Beef tenderloin.........5 to 6 lbs.	Carrot.........................1.
Bacon ....½ lb.	Stock........................2 glassesful.
Onions....................2.	Madeira ....1 glassful.

Time.—1 hour.

For the "Jardiniere" see No.

PREPARATION.—*To braise the tenderloin.* 1st. Lard 5 to 6 lbs. of tenderloin with about ½ lb. of bacon (cut in strips about ¼ of an inch thick). Place it in an oblong stove pan, sprinkle some salt over, add in the pan 2 onions and 1 carrot sliced, two glassesful stock, 1 glassful Madeira, let bake in an oven about 1 hour while basting frequently.

Gravy.—As indicated in No. 193.

Jardiniere.—See No. 324.

197. FILLET BRAISE RICHELIEU.

BRAISED TENDERLOIN RICHELIEU. (*Releve.*)

PROPORTIONS AND PREPARATION.—Same as for the above, No. 196 Served with a Richelieu as a garnish.

For the Richelieu see No 325.

198. FILLET BRAISE FINANCIERE.

BRAISED TENDERLOIN FINANCIERE. (*Releve.*)

PROPORTIONS AND PREPARATION.—Same as for No. 196. Served with a Financiere.

For the Financiere see No. 326.

199. FILLET BRAISE NAPOLITAINE.

BRAISED TENDERLOIN NAPOLITAINE. (*Releve.*)

PROPORTIONS AND PREPARATION.—Same as for No. 196. Serve with a Napolitaine and the gravy apart.

For the Napolitaine see No. 327.

200. ENTRECOTE MAITRE D'HOTEL.

BROILED STEAK A LA MAITRE D'HOTEL. (*Entree.*)

PROPORTIONS.—For five persons:

Steak..........3 to 4 lbs.	Parsley......................¼ handful.
Butter...........3 tablespoonsful.	*Time.*—15 minutes.

PREPARATION.—1st. Cut the steaks about one inch thick, let them broil on bright fire for about 5 minutes then turn them and let them broil again for 5 minutes. 2d. Put the steaks on a warm dish and place on each one about one-half tablespoonful butter, mixed with chopped parsley.

201. ENTRECOTE AU BEURRE D'ANCHOIS.

(Entree.)

PROPORTIONS AND PREPARATION.—Same as for the above, No. 200, but instead of mixing the butter with chopped parsley mix it in a mortar with 1 or 2 anchovies broken fine.

202. ENTRECOTE SOUBISE.

BROILED STEAK A LA SOUBISE. *(Entree.)*

PROPORTIONS AND PREPARATION.—1st. Same as for No. 200. 2d. Serve with a Soubise sauce (No. 315) apart.

203. ENTRECOTE BEARNAISE.

BROILED STEAK WITH BEARNASE SAUCE. *(Entree.)*

PROPORTIONS AND PREPARATION.—1st. As for No. 200. 2d. Serve with a Bearnaise sauce (No. 314) apart.

This is one of the most delicious dishes known among French cooks.

204. ENTRECOTE CREOLE.

BROILED STEAK WITH CREOLE SAUCE. *(Entree.)*

PROPORTIONS AND PREPARATION —1st Same as for No. 200. 2d. Serve Creole sauce (No. 319) apart.

205. ENTRECOTE A LA PARISIENNE.

BROILED STEAK A LA PARISIENNE. *(Entree.)*

PROPORTIONS AND PREPARATION.—1st. Same as for No. 200. 2d. Place the steaks in a warm dish and pour over them a sauce Parisienne, No. 316

206. ENTRECOTE BORDELAISE.

BROILED STEAK BORDELAISE. *(Entree.)*

PROPORTIONS AND PREPARATION.—1st. Same as for No. 200. 2d. Place the steaks in a warm dish and pour over a sauce Bordelaise, No. 317.

207. CHATAUBRIAND OR BEEFSTEAK* MAITRE D'HOTEL.

BEEFSTEAK A LA MAITRE D'HOTEL.

PROPORTIONS AND PREPARATION.—As for the Entrecote Maitre d'Hotel. No. 200.

208. CHATAUBRIAND OR BEEFSTEAK AU BEURRE D'ANCHOIS.

(*Entree.*)

PROPORTIONS AND PREPARATION.—As for the Entrecote au beurre d'anchois. No. 201, but use tenderloin instead of steak.

209. CHATAUBRIAND OR BEEFSTEAK SOUBISE.

(*Entree.*)

PROPORTIONS AND PREPARATION.—As for the Entrecote Soubise, No. 202, but use tenderloin instead of steak.

210. CHATAUBRIAND OR BEEFSTEAK BEARNAISE.

(*Entree.*)

PROPORTIONS AND PREPARATION.—As for the Entrecote Bearnaise, No. 203, but use tenderloin instead of steak.

211. CHATAUBRIAND OR BEEFSTEAK CREOLE.

(*Entree.*)

PROPORTIONS AND PREPARATION.—As for the Entrecote Sauce Creole, No. 204, but use tenderloin instead of steak.

212. CHATAUBRIAND OR BEEFSTEAK SAUCE PARISIENNE.

(*Entree.*)

PROPORTIONS AND PREPARATION.—As for the Entrecote Sauce Parisienne, No. 205, but use tenderloin instead of steak.

213. CHATAUBRIAND OR BEEFSTEAK BORDELAISE.

(*Entree.*)

PROPORTIONS AND PREPARATION.—As for the Entrecote Bordelaise, but use tenderloin instead of steak.

---

*Beefsteaks are slices of tenderloin from ¾ to 1 inch thick, and Chataubriand beefsteak two times as thick. Steaks, Chataubriand and beefsteak are especially breakfast and lunch dishes, and when served with Soubise or Bearnaise sauce are highly palatable. They should be served with fried potatoes.

214. BOEUF SAUTE A LA STROGONOFF.

BEEF SAUTE A LA STROGONOFF. (*Entree.*)

PROPORTIONS.—For five persons:

Beef (tenderloin, roll or steak)....2 lbs.
Onion....................1.
Butter.................3 tablespoonsful.
Flour........... ....1 tablespoonful.
Cream................2 glassesful.
Worcestershire sauce..............2 tablespoonsful.

Time.—25 minutes.

PREPARATION.—1st. Slice your beef in slices the size of a half dollar but twice as thick. 2d. Let brown 1 chopped onion in a sauce pan with 3 tablespoonsful butter, add the sliced meat and let fry for about 5 minutes. 3d. Sprinkle over 1 tablespoonful flour, 2 glassesful cream, 2 tablespoonsful Worcestershire Sauce. Add some chopped parsley, let cook awhile and serve in a warm hollow dish.

215. FILLET SAUTE AUX PETITS POIS.

TENDERLOIN WITH GREEN PEAS. (*Entree.*)

PROPORTIONS.—For five persons:

Tenderloin....3 lbs.
Butter ....3 tablespoonsful.
Flour.............1 tablespoonful.
Stock............⅛ glassful.

Time.—15 minutes.

PREPARATION.—1st. Slice the tenderloin about 1 inch thick. Let brown in butter in a shallow stew pan or a frying pan for five to ten minutes. Place them on a dish which you keep in a warm (but not hot) place. 2d. Add in the pan 1 tablespoonful flour, ⅛ glassful stock or water, let boil awhile and pour this sauce over the tenderloin steak. Serve with the French peas (No. 358) apart.

216. FILLET SAUTE AUX OLIVES.

TENDERLOIN STEAK WITH OLIVES. (*Entree.*)

PROPORTIONS.—For five persons:

Tenderloir...............3 lbs.
Olives............. ....About 24.
White wine............⅛ glassful.
Stock....................1 glassful.

Time.—20 minutes.

PREPARATION.—1st. Stone about 24 olives (pickled), dip them awhile in boiling water and let them drip. 2d. As indicated in 1st. in No. 215. 3d. Add in the same pan 1 tablespoonful flour, ⅛ glassful white wine, 1 glassful stock, and the olives, let boil for 5 minutes and pour over the tenderloin steaks.

217. FILLET SAUTE BORDELAISE.

TENDERLOIN STEAK BORDELAISE. (*Entree.*)

PROPORTIONS.—For five persons:

Tenderloin....3 lbs.	Echalotte ....2 pieces.
Butter..........2 tablespoonsful.	Parsley. ....½ handful.
Flour...........1 tablespoonful.	Red wine...............1 glassful.

Time.—15 minutes.

PREPARATION.—1st. As 1st. in No. 215. 2d. Add in the same pan 2 chopped echalottes; let brown awhile; sprinkle over one tablespoonful flour; add one glassful red wine; let boil for 5 minutes; add some chopped parsley and pour over the tenderloin steaks.

218. FILLET SAUTE A L'AMERICAINE.

TENDERLOIN STEAKS A L'AMERICAINE. (*Entree.*)

PROPORTIONS.—For five persons:

Tenderloin ....3 lbs.	Tomato catsup..........4 tablespoonsful.
Butter................2 tablespoonsful.	Worcestershire sauce.2 tablespoonsful.
Stock.................1 glassful.	*Time.*—15 minutes.

PREPARATION.—1st. As for No. 215. 2d. Pour in the same pan 4 tablespoonsful tomato catsup, 2 tablespoonsful Worcestershire sauce, 1 glassful stock; let boil for 5 minutes and pour over the tenderloin steak.

219. FILLET SAUTE AUX CHAMPIGNONS.

TENDERLOIN STEAK WITH MUSHROOMS. (*Entree.*)

PROPORTIONS.—For five persons:

Tenderloin....3 lbs.	Mushrooms......¼ lb.
Butter...........2 tablespoonsful.	Flour...............1 tablespoonful.

Time.—15 minutes.

PREPARATION.—1st. As in No. 215. 2d. Add in the pan ¼ lb. can of mushrooms (sliced) with their own juice, 1 tablespoonful flour; let brown awhile and pour on the tenderloin steaks.

220. FILLET SAUTE AUX TRUFFLES.

TENDERLOIN STEAK WITH TRUFFLES. (*Entree.*)

PROPORTIONS.—For five persons:

Tenderloin .....3 lbs.	Truffles...................¼ lb. can.
Butter............2 tablespoonsful.	Madeira..................1 glassful.
Flour...........1 tablespoonful.	*Time.*—15 minutes.

PREPARATION.—As for the above (No. 219), but instead of mushrooms use ¼ lb. can of truffles, and add 1 glassful Madeira.

221. FILLET SAUTE A LA MOELLE.

TENDERLOIN STEAK WITH MARROW. (*Entree.*)

PROPORTIONS.—For five persons:

Tenderloin.....3 lbs.	Flour.............1 tablespoonful.
Butter ....2 tablespoonsful.	Madeira........½ glassful
Marrow bones.1 or 2.	Stock............1 glassful.

Time.—20 minutes.

PREPARATION.—1st. Take the marrow out of one or two marrow bones; slice it about ¼ inch thick; dip these slices a little while in boiling water and let them drip. 2d. Same as 1st. in No. 215, but do not let the steak cook too much. 3d. Place the steaks on a warm dish, with the marrow slices over them. 4th. Add in the same sauce pan 1 tablespoonful flour, 1 glassful stock, ½ glassful Madeira; let boil awhile and pour over the tenderloin steak.

222. PETITS FILLETS ROSSINI.

(*Entree.*)

PROPORTIONS.—For five persons:

Tenderloin........3 lbs.	Madeira ....⅓ glassful.
Butter ....2 tablespoonsful.	Stock .... 1 glassful.
Paté de foie gras. ¼ to ⅓ lb.	*Time.*—20 minutes.

PREPARATION.—1st. As indicated in No. 215, but don't let them cook too much. 2d. Dispose the steaks on a warm dish and place over each a slice of paté de foie gras; keep the dish in a warm but not hot place for awhile. 3d. Add in the same pan 1 tablespoonful flour, ⅓ glassful Madeira, 1 glassful stock, ⅛ can truffles sliced quite fine or cut in dices, with their own juice; let boil awhile and pour over the tenderloin steaks.

223. BITOCKS A LA RUSSE.

(*Entree.*)

PROPORTIONS.—For five persons:

Beef (shoulder pieces)2 lbs.	Flour.............4 tablespoonsful.
Bread crumbs ....1 lb.	Worcestershire
Butter ....¼ lb.	sauce ....1 tablespoonful.
Milk ....1 glassful.	*Time.*—¼ hour.

PREPARATION.—Chop the meat; mix it well with one-half pound bread crumbs which have been soaked in 1 pint milk till soft. 2d. Divide that pap in cakes (about six for each pound); roll them in flour, giving the form of beefsteak; let them fry in butter for 10 minutes, and place them on a warm dish.   3d Add in the pan 2 tablespoonsful flour, 1 pint milk, 1 tablespoonful Worcestershire sauce; let boil awhile.   4th. Pour this sauce over the meat and let bake in an oven until light brown.

224. STRAZI A LA POLONAISE.

(*Entree.*)

PROPORTIONS.—For five persons:

Beef (steak)...2 lbs.	Stock ....2 glassesful.
Sausage meat 1 lb.	Carrots ....,2.
Butter ....2 tablespoonsful.	Onions ....2.
Madeira........1 glassful.	Salt and pepper..To suit the taste.

Time.—2¼ hours.

PREPARATION.—1st. Slice the meat the size of the hand and about ⅓ of an inch thick.   2d. Chop the sausage meat with one-half handful parsley; place about 2 tablespoonsful on a piece of meat; roll them in the shape of small cylinder and tie both ends with a little thread.   3d. Let them brown awhile in butter in a shallow stew pan, then add 1 glassful Madeira, 2 glassesful stock, 2 carrots and 2 onions sliced; salt and pepper to suit the taste; cover the pan and let cook for about 2 hours. 4th. When ready to serve place them on a warm dish, cut the thread off, the pieces remaining rolled; pass the juice through a sifter and pour over the meat; serve with mashed potatoes apart.

225. BŒUF A LA MODE.

BEEF A LA MODE. (*Entree.*)

PROPORTIONS.—For five persons*:

Beef (shoulder, rump, round, etc.).........5 to 6 lbs.	Carrots......................3
Calf's feet...............2.	Small onions ....6.
Veal knuckle ....1.	Parsley..... ....⅛ lb.
White wine...........1 glassful.	Thyme and laurel......A little.
Fat or lard..............2 tablespoonsful.	Salt and pepper.........To suit taste.
	Time.—5 hours.

PREPARATION.—1st. Warm two tablespoonsful fat or lard in a shallow stew pan, and brown the meat till well colored on both sides.   2d. Add one glassful stock or water, 3 carrots cut in four endwise, 6 small onions, ¼ handful parsley tied with some thyme and laurel, also one glassful wine, white preferred, two calf's feet cut in four and 1 veal knuckle (these are to make an unctuous sauce).   3d. Bake in an oven slowly for five hours, turning and basting the meat from time to time.   4th. Skim the floating grease off and serve with a vegetable in a hollow dish.

---

*The beef a la mode may be warmed over; therefore it is better to prepare it in quite a large quantity.

226. CULOTTE DE BŒUF A LA FLAMANDE.

BEEF ROUND A LA FLAMANDE. (*Entree.*)

PROPORTIONS.—For five persons*:

Beef round or mouse..15 to 20 lbs.   Celery stalk ....1.
Carrots ....3.   Onions ....3.

Time.—5½ hours.

For the Flamande see No. 329.

PREPARATION.—1st. Bone a 15 to 20 lb. piece of beef round; tie it with a twine and put it in a kettle with the bones and enough cold water to cover it well; let it boil while skimming, and when the stock is clear add 6 carrots, 1 celery stalk, 3 onions (one having been halved and browned on the range); let cook slowly for 5 hours, as indicated for the stock soup No. 1. 4th. Place the beef in a long dish, with a "Flamande" No. 329 as a garnish, and serve with a tomato sauce apart.

227. CULOTTE DE BŒUF A L'ANGLAISE.

BEEF ROUND A L'ANGLAISE. (*Entree*)

As for the above, but serve with boiled potatoes and a horseradish sauce.

228. EMINCE DE BŒUF A LA BOURGEOISE.

MINCED BEEF A LA BOURGEOISE. (*Entree.*)

PROPORTIONS.—For five persons:

Boiled beef.....2 lbs.   Onion...................1.
Butter..... ......1 tablespoonful.   Stock..... ....1 glassful.
Flour ....1 tablespoonful.   White wine..........1 glassful.
Bread crumbs.2 tablespoonsful.   Parsley................¼ handful.

Time —⅓ hour.

PREPARATION.—Slice the boiled beef quite fine, place it in a hollow dish. 2d. Fry one chopped onion in butter for 5 minutes, sprinkle over some chopped parsley and 1 tablespoonful flour, stir well the whole, add 1 glassful white wine and 1 glassful stock. Let boil awhile and pour over the beef. 3d. Sprinkle some bread crumbs over and let bake in an oven for ¼ of an hour

229. BŒUF EN MIROTON.

BEEF WITH ONIONS. (*Entree.*)

PROPORTIONS.—For five persons:

Boiled beef......2 lbs.   Flour...................1 tablespoonful.
Onions..........12.   Stock...... ....2 glassesful.
Butter... ....3 tablespoonsful.   Salt and pepper.....To suit taste.

Time.—1¼ hours.

*By following these proportions you will have certainly too much meat for 5 persons, but the cold beef may be used afterwards as indicated following and you will obtain in the same time a fine stock.

PREPARATION.—1st. Slice the beef quite fine and place it in a hollow dish. 2d. Slice the onions and let them cook in a stew pan with 3 tablespoonsful butter till light brown. Sprinkle over 1 tablespoonful flour, add 2 glassesful stock, and let boil awhile. 3d. Pour over the beef and let bake for 1 hour in an oven.

230. CROQUETTES DE BŒUF.

BEEF CROQUETTES. (*Entree.*)

PROPORTIONS.—For five persons:

Boiled beef...2 lbs.	Flour.................4 tablespoonsful.
Onions.........3.	Salt and pepper...To suit the taste.
Eggs............3.	Lard or fat enough to fry.
Butter..........4 tablespoonsful.	*Time.*—¾ hour.

PREPARATION.—1st. Chop the beef very fine. 2d. Chop the onions. Let them brown in a sauce pan with 2 tablespoonsful butter and pour them in a large mixing bowl with the chopped meat, 6 boiled potatoes (peeled) also 3 eggs (broken as indicated No.   ), some salt and pepper, mix well the whole. 3d. Divide into croquettes about 4 inches long and 1½ inches thick. Roll them in flour and let fry. Serve with a tomato sauce apart. (No. 318.)

231. BŒUF FROID SAUCE VINAIGRETTE.

COLD BEEF WITH SAUCE VINAIGRETTE. (*Entree.*)

PROPORTIONS.—For five persons:

Cold boiled beef......... ....2 lbs.

For Vinaigrette Sauce see No. 166.

PREPARATION.—Slice the beef, place it in a hollow dish and pour a Vinaigrette Sauce No. 166 over it.

232. SALADE DE BŒUF.

BEEF SALAD. (*Entree.*)

PROPORTIONS.—For five persons:

Cold boiled beef......2 lbs.	Oil....... ....4 tablespoonsful.
Hard boiled eggs .....4.	Vinegar..............2 tablespoonsful.
Green onion............1.	Salt and pepper...........To suit the
Parsley..................½ handful.	taste.

PREPARATION.—1st. Slice the beef, put in a salad dish with four hard boiled eggs sliced, one green onion chopped, 4 tablespoonsful oil, 2 tablespoonsful vinegar, salt and pepper to suit the taste, sprinkle over some chopped parsley and stir the whole. You may add also sliced tomatoes and sliced cucumbers, etc.

233. BEEF STEAK PIE.

(*Entree.*)

PROPORTIONS.—For five persons:

Beef tenderloin	4 to 5 lbs.	Egg	1.
Flour	1 lb.	Stock	1 glassful.
Butter	6 tablespoonsful.	Worcestershire sauce..1 tablespoonful.	
Water	1 glassful.		
Onion	2 pieces.	Salt and pepper	To suit the taste.
Potatoes	6.		
Hard boiled eggs	3.	*Time.*—1½ hour.	

PREPARATION.—1st. Make a pie paste with 1 lb. flour, 4 tablespoonsful butter, 1 glassful water and a little salt; divide this dough in 2 parts and roll both quite thin. 2d. Place one half in a baking dish or tin, taking care that the dough falls over the edge about ½ inch (to be folded after over the upper crust of the pie). 3d. Cook the tenderloin as indicated in No. 215, and when half cooked place in the baking dish with 3 hard boiled eggs sliced, 6 boiled potatoes sliced. 4th. Put in the pan in which this has been fried 1 glass stock, 1 tablespoonful Worcestershire sauce, some salt and pepper, stir well the whole and pour over the steaks. 5th. Place the upper crust, fold the edges of the lower crust over the edge of the upper, make a slit in the middle of the crust, brush with a beaten egg, and bake for about one hour.

234. LANGUE DE BŒUF SAUCE PIQUANTE.

(*Entree.*)

PROPORTIONS.—For five persons:

Beef tongue	1.	Celery	1 stalk.
Carrots	2.	*Time.* { To freshen...4 hours.	
Onions	2.	{ To cook ......4 hours.	

PREPARATION.—1st. Freshen the tongue in fresh water for about 4 hours (water should be changed at least four times). 2d. Place the tongue in a kettle with enough cold water to cover it well, add 3 carrots, 2 onions, 1 stalk of celery, all these sliced, let cook for 4 hours. 3d. Dip the tongue in cold water, skin it, put it again in the stock in which it has been cooked and as soon as it is warm place it in a warm dish with green parsley around and serve with a sauce piquante apart No. 321.

235. LANGUE FROIDE.

COLD SALTED OR SMOKED TONGUE.

PROPORTIONS AND PREPARATION.—Freshen, cook and skin the tongue as above and serve cold for breakfast, lunch or picnic.

236. SANDWICHES A LA LANGUE.

TONGUE SANDWICHES. (*Entree.*)

PROPORTIONS.—For 10 sandwiches:

Tongue..............1 lb.	Salt and pepper...To suit the taste.
Butter.............5 tablespoonsful.	Cayenne pepper...A little.
Mustard...........1 tablespoonful.	Bread ....20 slices.

PREPARATION.—Make a dressing by mixing 5 tablespoonsful butter with 1 tablespoonful mustard, salt and pepper to suit the taste, a little cayenne pepper. Trim the crust from 20 slices bread, butter them with the dressing and lay between every two some slices of cold tongue.

237. SANDWICH AU ROSBIF.

BEEF SANDWICH.

PROPORTIONS AND PREPARATION.—As for No. 236, but use cold roast beef instead of tongue.

238. CERVELLES DE BŒUF A LA POULETTE.

BEEF BRAIN A LA POULETTE. (*Entree.*)

PROPORTIONS.—For five persons:

Beef brains............3 or 4.	Milk ....2 tablespoonsful.
Onion....................1.	Butter ....4 tablespoonsful.
Parsley...................¼ handful.	Flour.............1 tablespoonful.
Yolks of eggs........2.	Vinegar ....⅛ glassful.

Time.—¾ hour.

PREPARATION.—1st. Take the skins off the brains and let them freshen from 3 to 4 hours in cold water, change every hour. 2d. Cut the brains in two, place them in a stew pan with one sliced onion, ⅛ glassful of vinegar, some salt and pepper, and enough cold water to cover them well. Let cook half an hour. 3d. Let them drip, cut each half in four and place in a warm, hollow dish, which you keep in a warm place. 4th. Melt in another sauce pan 2 tablespoonsful butter, mixed with one tablespoonful flour. Mix well with one glassful of water, in which the brain has been cooked. Let boil awhile, then add some chopped parsley and when ready to serve, place the sauce pan on the corner of the range, add 2 tablespoonsful butter, mix it with 2 yolks of eggs and 2 tablespoonsful milk. Do not let boil again and pour over the brains.

239. CERVELLES AU BEURRE NOIR.

BEEF BRAIN WITH BROWN BUTTER. (*Entree.*)

PROPORTIONS.—For five persons:

Brains.......................3 to 4.	Parsley..................¼ handful.
Butter.....................¼ lb.	Vinegar.................¼ glassful.

PREPARATION.—Nos. 1, 2 and 3 as above, No. 238. 4th. Melt in a frying pan ⅛ lb. butter. Let warm till light brown. Add the chopped parsley, and as soon as this last is fried, pour the whole over the brain, then (and not before)* pour ¼ glass of vinegar in the pan, stir awhile, and pour also over the brain.

VEAL.

To be good veal should be at the same time white and quite fat and it then constitutes very delicate and palatable dishes.

Do not forget that veal like all young animals ought to be thoroughly cooked or it is unwholesome.

240. LONGE DE VEAU ROTI.

ROAST LOIN OF VEAL. (*Roast.*)

PROPORTIONS.—For 10 persons:

Veal loin ....8 to 9 lbs. Onion............................1.
Carrot.....................1. Water........................1 glassful.
Time.—2 hours.

PREPARATION.—1st. Take the kidney or the kidney fat off, roll it lengthwise and tie it with twine. Place it in a pan with 1 onion and 1 carrot sliced, sprinkle some salt over, add one glassful water and let bake in an oven while basting for two hours. 2d. Cut the twine off and place in a long warm dish and serve the gravy apart (No. 193) in a sauce bowl.

241. LONGE DE VEAU JARDINIERE.

LOIN OF VEAL JARDINIERE. (*Releve.*)

PROPORTIONS AND PREPARATION.—Prepare the loin as indicated above No. 240, and do as indicated for the braised tenderloin jardiniere.

242. LONGE DE VEAU A LA CREME.

LOIN OF VEAL WITH CREAM. (*Releve or Entree.*)

PROPORTIONS:

Veal loin........8 to 9 lbs. Milk.....................1 or 1½ pints.
Butter............2 tablespoonsful. Grated cheese.........¼ lb.
Flour...... ....3 tablespoonsful. Salt and pepper...To suit the taste.
Time.—2 hours.

PREPARATION.—Roast the loin as indicated, No. 240, and during that time prepare a cream sauce as follows. 1st. Melt in a sauce pan two tablespoonsful butter and mix with two tablespoonsful flour. Add salt

* If you pour vinegar in warm butter you will have an explosion and be soiled if not badly burned.

and pepper to suit the taste, 1 or 1½ pint milk, boil five or six minutes while stirring continually; when the sauce is quite thick place it aside in a warm but not too hot place. 2d. Half an hour before serving carve the loin in slices about ⅔ inch thick, then reconstruct the whole loin by placing sauce between its slices. Pour the remaining portion of the sauce over, sprinkle the grated cheese on this and bake in an oven and serve with a gravy apart. (No. 193.)

245. VEAU A LA BOURGEOISE.

VEAL A LA BOURGEOISE. (*Entree.*)

PROPORTIONS.

Veal champ end. 3 to 4 lbs.	Small onions.............................12.
Butter............2 tablespoonsful.	Carrots .... 6.
Stock or water...2 glassesful.	*Time.*—1½ hours.

PREPARATION.—Place the veal in a stew pan with 2 tablespoonsful butter. Let brown awhile, add 2 glassesful stock, 6 carrots cut in four, 12 small onions, and let cook slowly while basting one hour and one half. 2d. Serve the veal with a vegetable around it, skin the floating grease off the gravy and serve it apart in a sauce bowl.

244. PORTRINE DE VEAU FARCIE.

STUFFED VEAL BRISKET. (*Entree.*)

PROPORTIONS.

Veal brisket............4 to 5 lbs.	Butter................1 tablespoonful.
Water...........................1 glassful.	

FOR THE STUFFING:

Sausage meat.............. 1 lb.	Butter.................1 tablespoonful.
Bread crumbs..............½ pint.	Parsley................¼ handful.
Onion.......................1.	Salt and pepper......To suit taste.
Time.—¾ hour.	

PREPARATION.—1st. Take from 4 to 5 lbs. veal brisket, prepare to be stuffed* and stuff it with a stuffing made as indicated below. 2d. Sew the brisket with a needle, place it in a pan with 2 tablespoonsful butter over it, add one glassful water, and let bake as indicated, No. 240. Serve with the gravy apart.

STUFFING.—Let brown one chopped onion in some butter and mix it with the bread crumbs (having been dipped wet in one half pint milk) and chopped parsley, add the sausage meat chopped fine and mix well the whole.

---

*Veal brisket are sold by butchers already prepared for stuffing.

245. BLANQUETTE DE VEAU.

BLANQUETTE OF VEAL. (*Entree.*)

PROPORTIONS.

Veal brisquet.........5 to 6 lbs.	Butter................2 tablespoonful.
Onion......... ....1.	Flour.....................1 tablespoonful.
Carrot......... ....1.	Salt and pepper......To suit taste.
Parsley...................¼ handful.	*Time.*—2 hours.

PREPARATION.—1st. Cut the brisket in pieces about 3 inches long and 1¼ inches wide. Freshen them in cold water for one quarter of an hour. 2d. Place them in a stew pan, cover them with cold water, let boil and when it begins to boil add 2 onions, 2 carrots sliced, one handful parsley, tied with a thread, salt and pepper (white). Allow to cook for 1½ hours. When the veal is cooked melt in another sauce pan two tablespoonsful butter, mix it with one tablespoonsful flour, add little by little and while stirring enough of the stock in which the veal has been cooked to obtain quite a strong sauce. Place the cooked veal (but not the vegetables) in the second stew pan, boil the whole together and when ready to serve place the sauce pan on the corner of the range and pour in 4 eggs mixed with 2 tablespoonsful milk and serve with rice a la Georgienne apart. (No. 406.)

246. VEAU A LA PROVENCALE.

VEAL A LA PROVENCALE. (*Entree.*)

PROPORTIONS.—For five persons:

Veal brisket...5 to 6 lbs.	White wine.........1 pint.
Onion............1.	Tomato catsup......2 tablespoonsful.
Garlic cloves...1.	Parsley............ ....¼ handful.
Flour............1 tablespoonful.	Olive oil..............3 tablespoonsful.
	Time.—1¾ hours.

PREPARATION.—1st. As 1st. No. 245. 2d. Warm in a stew pan 3 tablespoonsful olive oil, add the veal and let brown. 3d. Add 1 chopped onion, 1 crushed garlic clove, sprinkle over 1 tablespoonful flour, 1 pint white wine, 2 tablespoonsful tomato catsup, some salt and parsley, cook for 1½ hours. 4th. When ready to serve, skim the floating grease off, sprinkle over some chopped parsley, and serve in a warm hollow dish.

247. COTELETTE DE VEAU GRILLEE.

BROILED VEAL CHOP. (*Entree.*)

PROPORTIONS.—For five persons:

Veal chops......... ....6 to 8.	Bread crumbs.3 to 4 tablespoonsful.
Butter...................... ......¼ lb.	Parsley..........¼ handful.
	Time.—15 minutes.

PREPARATION.—Dip the chops in melted butter, roll them in bread crumbs and let them brown on slow fire. Serve with a Maitre d'Hotel, No. 200.

248. COTELETTE DE VEAU AUX PETITS POIS.

VEAL CHOPS WITH FRENCH PEAS. (*Entree.*)

PROPORTIONS.—For five persons:

Veal chops	6 to 8.	French peas	No. 422.
Butter	¼ lb.	*Time.*—20 minutes.	

PREPARATION.—1st. Let melt ¼ lb. butter in a shallow stew pan, fry the chops for about 20 minutes turning them frequently.   2d. Place those chops on a warm dish, pour over the sauce in which they have been fried and serve with the French peas (No. 358) apart.

249. COTELETTE DE VEAU JARDINIERE.

VEAL CHOPS JARDINIERE. (*Entree.*)

PROPORTIONS AND PREPARATION.—As for the above, No. 248.   Serve with a jardiniere (No. 324) apart.

250. COTELETTES DE VEAU AUX EPINARDS.

VEAL CHOPS WITH SPINAGE. (*Entree.*)

PROPORTIONS AND PREPARATION.—As for the above, No. 248.   Serve with spinage (No. 365) apart.

251. COTELETTES DE VEAU SAUCE TOMATE.

VEAL CHOPS WITH TOMATO SAUCE. (*Entree.*)

PROPORTIONS AND PREPARATION.—As for the above.   Serve with a tomato sauce (No. 318) apart.

252. COTELETTES DE VEAU AUX CHAMPIGNONS.

VEAL CHOPS WITH MUSHROOMS. (*Entree.*)

PROPORTIONS.—For five persons:

Veal chops	6 to 8.	Flour	2 tablespoonsful.
Butter	¼ lb.	White wine	½ glassful.
	Time.— ½ hour.		

PREPARATION.—1st. As 1st. No. 248.   Dispose the chops in a warm dish and add in the same saucepan 2 tablespoonsful flour, stir well, add ½ glass white wine, ¼ lb. can mushrooms (minced), with their juice, let boil awhile and pour over the chops.

253. COTELETTES DE VEAU AUX TRUFFLES.

VEAL CHOPS WITH TRUFFLES. (*Entree.*)

PROPORTIONS AND PREPARATION.—As for No. 252, but replace the mushrooms with ⅛ can truffles and the white wine with madeira.

254. COTELETTE DE VEAU MILANAISE.

VEAL CHOPS A LA MILANAISE. (*Entree.*)

PROPORTIONS.—For five persons:

Veal chops ....6 to 8.	Eggs............................2.
Bread crumbs...............2 to 3.	Butter .... .¼ lb.
Cheese ....¼ lb.	

PREPARATION.—1st. Dip the chops in beaten eggs, roll them in bread crumbs, mixed with rasped cheese and fry them in butter as indicated No. 248. 2d. Place the chops in a warm dish, pour over the butter in which they have been fried and serve with macaroni (Nos. 402-403) apart.

255. COTELETTES DE VEAU EN PAPILLOTTE.

VEAL CHOPS IN PAPILLOTTES. (*Entree.*)

 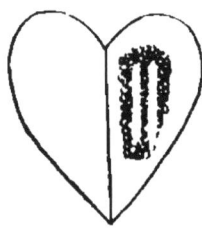 

PROPORTIONS AND PREPARATION.—Fry your chops as indicated No. 248, then do as indicated for the Herring in papillottes, No. 66.

1   II   III

256. ESCALOPPES DE VEAU GRILLEES MAITRE D'HOTEL.

ESCALLOPPES OF VEAL A LA MAITRE D'HOTEL. (*Entree.*)

PROPORTIONS —For five persons:

Veal chunk...2 to 3 lbs.	Bread crumbs.3 to 4 tablespoonsful.
Butter...........¼ lb.	Parsley..........¼ handful.

Time.—15 minutes.

PREPARATION.—1st. Slice the veal in pieces of the size of the hand and about ¾ inch thick. 2d. Do as indicated for the broiled veal chops No 247.

257. ESCALOPPES DE VEAU AUX PETITS POIS.

ESCALOPPES OF VEAL WITH FRENCH PEAS. (*Entree.*)

PROPORTIONS AND PREPARATION.—1st. As 1st No. 256. 2d. Do as indicated for the veal chops with French peas, No. 248.

258. ESCALLOPPE DE VEAU JARDINIERE.

ESCALOPPE OF VEAL JARDINIERE. (*Entree.*)

PROPORTIONS AND PREPARATION.—As for No. 257, and serve with a Jardiniere, No. 324, instead of French peas.

259. ESCALOPPE DE VEAU AUX EPINARDS.

ESCALOPPE OF VEAL WITH SPINAGE. (*Entree.*)

PROPORTIONS AND PREPARATION.—As for No. 257, but serve with spinage (No. 365) instead of French peas.

260. ESCALOPPE DE VEAU SAUCE TOMATE.

ESCALOPPE OF VEAL WITH TOMATO SAUCE. *Entree.*)

PROPORTIONS AND PREPARATION.—As for No. 257, but serve with tomato sauce apart, No. 318.

261. FOIE DE VEAU GRILLE.

BROILED VEAL LIVER. (*Entree.*)

PROPORTIONS.—For five persons:

Veal liver.................2 to 3 lbs.   Salt and pepper. To suit the taste.
Butter................¼ lb.   *Time.*—10 minutes.

PREPARATION.—1st. Take 2 to 3 lbs. veal liver (this should be of a clear and not dark color), slice in pieces of the size of the hand and about ¾ inch thick, dip it in melted butter, let broil on bright fire and serve with a Maitre d'Hotel. (No. 200.)

262. FOIE DE VEAU SAUTE AUX FINES HERBES.

VEAL LIVER SAUTE WITH PARSLEY. (*Entree.*)

PROPORTIONS.—For five persons:

Veal..............2 to 3 lbs.   Parsley ....⅛ handful.
Butter...........2 tablespoonsful. Salt and pepper. To suit the taste.
Time.—10 minutes.

PREPARATION.—1st. Slice the veal liver as indicated above, No. 261, and let it fry in butter in a shallow stew pan or frying pan. 2d. When ready to serve, sprinkle some chopped parsley over, place the slices in a warm dish and pour over the butter in which they have been fried.

263. FOIE DE VEAU SAUTE AU MADERE.

VEAL LIVER SAUTE WITH MADEIRA. (*Entree.*)

PROPORTIONS.—For five persons:

As above, No. 262, and ½ glassful Madeira, ⅓ glassful stock and 1 tablespoonful flour.

PREPARATION.—1st. As for No. 260. 2d. Sprinkle over 1 tablespoonful flour, add ⅓ glassful Madeira, ⅓ glassful stock, boil awhile, sprinkle over some parsley and serve in a hollow warm dish.

264. FOIE DE VEAU BONNE FEMME.

BACKED VEAL LIVER. (*Entree.*)

PROPORTIONS.—For five persons:

Veal liver......3 to 4 lbs.	Stock.........................⅓ glassful.
Bacon...........¼ lb.	Onion.........................1.
Butter...........2 tablespoonsful.	Carrots........................2.
White wine ...⅓ glassful.	Salt and pepper... To suit the taste.

Time —1⅓ hours.

PREPARATION.—1st. Lard the liver with ¼ lb. bacon, cut in long strips, place it in a stew pan and let it brown on both sides in 2 tablespoonsful butter. 2d. Add ⅓ glassful stock, ⅓ glassful white wine, some salt and pepper, 1 onion sliced, and 2 carrots cut in 4, cover the pan and let cook slowly while basting for about 1⅓ hours. 3d. Place it on a warm dish and pour the juice over through a sifter. Serve with mashed potatoes apart.

265. ROGNONS DE VEAU BROCHETTE.

BROILED VEAL KIDNEY. (*Entree.*)

PROPORTIONS.—For five persons:

Veal kidneys 6.	Lemon juice..............A little.
Butter.....3 to 4 tablespoonsful.	Salt and pepper.........To suit the
Parsley ...⅓ handful.	taste.

Time.—15 minutes.

PREPARATION.—1st. Cut each kidney in two parts endwise, in such a way as to open them but not to divide entirely and pass 2 wooden "brochettes" through them to keep them flat. 2d. Sprinkle some salt and pepper over them, dip them in melted butter and let broil on bright fire. 3d. Serve with a Maitre d'Hotel, No. 200, in which you have added a little lemon juice.

266. ROGNONS SAUTES AU MADERE.

KIDNEY SAUTE WITH MADEIRA. (*Entree.*)

PROPORTIONS AND PREPARATION.—As for the veal liver with Madeira, No. 263.

267. LANGUE DE VEAU SAUCE PIQUANTE.

VEAL TONGUE WITH SAUCE PIQUANTE. (*Entree.*)

PROPORTIONS AND PREPARATION. - As for the beef tongue sauce piquante, No. 234.

268. RIZ DE VEAU A LA FINANCIERE.

SWEET BREADS A LA FINANCIERE. (*Entree.*)

PROPORTIONS.—For five persons:

Sweet breads	4 lbs.	Carrots	2.
Onions	2.	Stock	2 glassesful.

Financiere, No. 241.

Time.— { To freshen........1 hour.
         { To blanche........10 minutes.
         { To cook...... ......1 hour.

PREPARATION.—1st. Take 4 lbs. sweet breads, let them freshen for 1 hour in cold water. 2d. Dip them in boiling water for 5 minutes and then in cold water, let them drip well (press them a little to drip thoroughly). 3d. Place in a shallow stew pan with 2 onions, 2 carrots, sliced, place the sweet breads over, add 2 glassesful stock and let bake for 1 hour in an oven, while basting from time to time. 4th. Place them in crown in a warm dish and serve with a financiere, No. 326, in the middle.

269. RIZ DE VEAU AUX EPINARDS.

SWEET BREADS WITH SPINAGE. (*Entree*)

PROPORTIONS AND PREPARATION.—1st., 2d., and 3d. as above, No. 268. 4th.   Place the sweet bread in a warm dish, pour over the sauce in which they have been cooked through a strainer, after having skimmed the floating grease off and serve with the spinage (No. 355) apart.

270. RIZ DE VEAU SAUCE TOMATE.

SWEET BREAD WITH TOMATO SAUCE. (*Entree*)

As for the above, No. 269, but serve with a tomato sauce apart.

271. CERVELLES DE VEAU A LA POULETTE.

VEAL BRAINS A LA POULETTE. (*Entree.*)

As for the beef brains a la poulette, No. 238.

272. CERVELLES DE VEAU AU BEURRE NOIR.

VEAL-BRAINS WITH BROWNED BUTTER.

As for the beef brains with browned butter, No. 239.

273. TETE DE VEAU VINAIGRETTE.

CALF HEAD WITH VINAIGRETTE SAUCE. (*Entree.*)

PROPORTIONS.—For five persons:

Calf head........¼.	Vinegar.................¼ glassful.
Flour ....2 tablespoonsful.	Water...................¼ gallon.
Onions..........2.	Vinaigrette sauce....No. 165.
Carrots..........3.	

PREPARATION.—1st. Cook the calf head as indicated in 1st., 2d. and 3d., No. 15 (turtle soup), and serve with a vinaigrette sauce (No. 165) apart.

274. TETE DE VEAU SAUCE TOMATE.

CALF HEAD WITH TOMATO SAUCE. (*Entree.*)

PROPORTIONS AND PREPARATION.—As for the above, No. 273, but serve with a tomato sauce (No. 318) apart.

275. TETE DE VEAU SAUCE PIQUANTE.

CALF HEAD WITH SAUCE PIQUANTE. (*Entree.*)

PROPORTIONS AND PREPARATION.—As for the above, No. 273, but serve with a sauce piquante (No. 321) apart.

276. PIEDS DE VEAU A LA POULETTE.

CALF FEET A LA POULETTE. (*Entree.*)

PROPORTIONS AND PREPARATION.—For five persons:—1st. Cook the feet (4 for 5 persons) as it is indicated for the calf's head. 2d. Take the bone off and prepare them a la poulette as indicated (No. 238) for the brains a la poulette.

277. PIEDS DE VEAU SAUCE TOMATE.

CALF FEET WITH TOMATO SAUCE. (*Entree.*)

PREPARATION.—1st. As for the above, No. 274. 2d. Take the bones off and serve warm with a tomato sauce (No. 321) apart.

278. PIEDS DE VEAU A LA VINAIGRETTE.

CALF FEET A LA VINAIGRETTE. (*Entree.*)

PREPARATION.—1st. and 2d. As for the above, No. 275, but serve cold with a vinaigrette sauce (No. 166).

MUTTON.

279. SELLE DE MOUTON A L'ANGLAISE.

SADDLE OF MUTTON ROASTED. (*Roast.*)

PROPORTIONS.—For 10 persons:
Saddle................12 to 15 lbs.
Water.................1 glassful.
Salt and pepper ..To suit the taste.
Time.—1 hour.

PREPARATION.—1st. Trim the grease and take off a kind of membranous skin which covers the back of the saddle: place it in a stove pan; sprinkle over some salt; add 1 glassful water and let bake in an oven for 1 hour as indicated for the roast beef, No. 193. Serve with potatoes fried in butter and the gravy apart.

280. SELLE DE MOUTON JARDINIERE.

SADDLE OF MUTTON JARDINIERE. (*Releve.*)

PROPORTIONS AND PREPARATION.—Roast the saddle as above, No. 279, and do as indicated for the Fillet Braise Jardiniere, No. 196.

281. SELLE DE MOUTON RICHELIEU.

SADDLE OF MUTTON RICHELIEU. (*Releve.*)

PROPORTIONS AND PREPARATION.—Roast the saddle as above, No. 279, and do as indicated for the Fillet Braise Richelieu, No. 197.

282. GIGOT DE MOUTON A LA FRANCAISE.

LEG OF MUTTON A LA FRANCAISE. (*Roast.*)

PROPORTIONS.—For five persons:*

Leg of mutton..........7 to 8 lbs.   Garlic cloves..........2 (if liked).
Time.—About 1½ hours.†

---

* The leg of mutton may be served cold for breakfast or lunches.
† 15 minutes roasting for every pound.

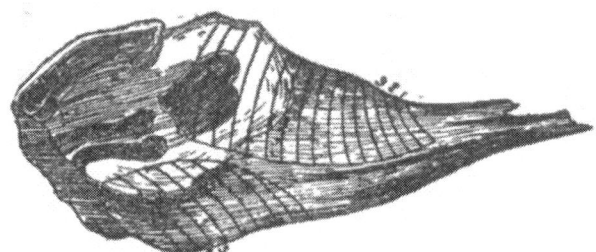

PREPARATION. — Pare the mutton leg and let it roast as indicated for the roast beef, No. 193, and serve with potatoes fried in butter or a salad.

NOTE.—In France we insert 2 or 3 garlic cloves in the meat in the portion near the handle.

283. GIGOT DE MOUTON A LA BRETONNE.

LEG OF MUTTON A LA BRETONNE. (*Entree.*)

PROPORTIONS AND PREPARATION.—As for the above, No. 282, and serve with kidney beans a la Bretonne, No. 330.

284. GIGOT DE MOUTON BOUILLI A L'ANGLAISE.

BOILED LEG OF MUTTON. (*Entree.*)

PROPORTIONS.—For five persons:

Leg of mutton..........7 to 8 lbs.   *Time.*—1¾ to 2 hours.

PREPARATION.—1st. The leg being prepared as above, No. 282, tie it in a napkin in a kettle with salted *boiling* water* and let it boil without interruption 15 minutes for each pound of meat. Serve with boiled potatoes apart.

285. GIGOT DE MOUTON BOUILLI SAUCE AUX CAPRES.

BOILED LEG OF MUTTON WITH CAPER SAUCE. (*Entree.*)

PROPORTIONS AND PREPARATION.—As for the above, No. 284, and serve with a caper sauce, No. 152.

286. GIGOT D'AGNEAU SAUCE MENTHE.

LEG OF LAMB, MINT SAUCE. (*Roast.*)

PROPORTIONS.—For five persons:

Leg of lamb............5 to 6 lbs.   *Time.*—1¼ to 1½ hours.

PREPARATION.—Roast the leg as indicated No. 282 and serve with a mint sauce apart, No. 323.

---

*There should be enough water so that the immersion of the leg will not stop the ebullition. If the ebullition is stopped the leg will not retain its juice.

287. EPAULE DE MOUTON A LA BONNE FEMME.

MUTTON SHOULDER A LA BONNE FEMME.   (*Family Roast.*)

PROPORTIONS.—For five persons:

Mutton shoulder ....4 to 5 lbs.	Potatoes..............About 2 doz.
Onions...........................2.	Salt and pepper...To suit the taste.

PREPARATION.—1st. Place the shoulder on a stove pan and around it the onions and potatoes; add 1 glassful water; sprinkle over some salt and pepper and let roast as indicated, No. 279. 2d. Serve in a warm dish, with the potatoes around, and pour the gravy over the meat.

288. EPAULE DE MOUTON FARCIE.

STUFFED MUTTON SHOULDER.   (*Roast or Entree.*)

PROPORTIONS.—For five persons:

Mutton shoulder......4 to 5 lbs.	Stuffing................See No. 244.

Time.—1 hour.

PREPARATION.—Take the bones off and stuff as indicated, No. 244. 2d. Let roast as indicated, No. 193, for about 1 hour. Serve with potatoes roasted in butter or mashed.

289. BLANQUETTE D'AGNEAU.

BLANQUETTE OF LAMB.   (*Entree.*)

PROPORTIONS AND PREPARATION.—As for No. 245, but replace the veal brisket by lamb brisket, which you cut in pieces ¼ of the size of the hand.

290. RAGOUT DE MOUTON.

FRENCH MUTTON STEW.   (*Entree.*)

PROPORTIONS.—For five persons:

Mutton brisket...7 to 8 lbs.	Onions.....................12.
Fat or lard........1 tablespoonful.	Potatoes....................24.
Flour...............1 tablespoonful.	Parsley....... ....½ handful.

Time.—1½ hours.

PREPARATION.—1st. Cut the mutton in pieces ⅓ the size of the hand; place it in a stew pan with 1 tablespoonful fat, and brown awhile. 2d. Add 1 tablespoonful flour; mix well and add just enough stock or water to cover the meat. 3d. Let boil while skimming for about ¼ hour; add 12 small onions, ⅓ handful parsley (tied with a thread); let boil again ½ hour. 4th. Add 24 potatoes cut in 2 or in 4 according to the size; cook again slowly for ½ hour and serve in a hollow dish. (Don't forget it takes more time to cook onions than potatoes.)

291. RAGOUT DE MOUTON A L'IRLANDAISE.

IRISH STEW. (*Entree.*)

PROPORTIONS.—For five persons:

Mutton brisket.........7 to 8 lbs. Potatoes...........2 doz.
Onions.....................12. Flour. ....3 tablespoonsful.
Parsley...... ....⅛ handful. Stock or water...2 glassesful.

Time.—1¼ hours.

PREPARATION.—1st. Cut the meat as No. 290; place it in a stew pan; add enough water to cover it well, and skim while boiling. 2d. Add 12 small onions, ⅛ handful parsley (tied), and cook for ½ hour. 3d. Add 3 tablespoonsful flour beaten in a bowl with 2 glassesful stock or water, and the potatoes cut in 2 or 4, and cook again for ⅛ hour.

292. COTELETTES DE MOUTON GRILLEES A LA FRANCAISE.

FRENCH MUTTON CHOPS BROILED. (*Entree.*)

PROPORTIONS.—For five persons:

French mutton chops.....6 to 8. *Time.*—10 minutes.

NOTE.—French chops are small rib chops, the end of the bone having been trimmed off, the fat cut away from the end, leaving the round piece of meat attached to the large end.

PREPARATION.—Broil the chops on bright fire, taking care to turn them frequently; serve with potatoes fried in butter, mashed potatoes or French peas, etc.

293. COTELETTES DE MOUTON PANEES.

MUTTON CHOPS WITH BREAD CRUMBS. (*Entree.*)

PROPORTIONS.—For five persons:

Mutton chops..6 to 8. Bread crumbs..2 to 3 tablespoonsful.
Butter...........2 to 3 tablespoonsful. *Time.*—15 minutes.

PREPARATION.—Dip the chops in melted butter; roll them in bread crumbs and let broil on not too bright fire.

294. COTELETTES DE MOUTON A L'ANGLAISE.

ENGLISH MUTTON CHOPS. (*Entree.*)

PROPORTIONS.

English chops...............5 to 6. *Time.*—20 minutes.

NOTE.—English chops are thicker than the former, No. 292, and are cut from loin or tenderloin and trimmed into a nice shape.

PREPARATION.—As for the above, 292.

295. SHACHLICK DE MOUTON A LA CIRCASSIENNE.

BROCHETTES OF MUTTON A LA CIRCASSIENNE. (*Entree.*)

NOTE.—This is the national dish of the Circassians.

PROPORTIONS.

Mutton (loin, leg or shoulder)..3 lbs.   Butter.. ....3 tablespoonsful.

Time.—15 minutes.

PREPARATION.—1st. Cut the mutton in slices about 2¼ inches square and ⅜ inch thick; spit them on wooden brochettes (or on silver bro_chettes); dip them in melted butter and broil them on bright fire while turning; serve with rice a la Georgienne.

296, 297, 298, 299, 300.—For mutton kidneys, brains and feet, do as indicated for veal kidneys, brains and feet, Nos. 265, 266, 267, 268, 269.

PORK.

301. JAMBON FROID.

COLD HAM.

PROPORTIONS.—For five persons:

Ham ....10 to 12 lbs.	Carrots...........................2 or 3.
Onions ....2 or 3.	Celery.........................2 stalks.

Time.— { To freshen.........3 to 4 hours.
{ To cook ....5 to 6 hours.

PREPARATION.—*How to cook a ham*: 1st. Freshen the ham in cold water from 3 to 4 hours. 2d. Place it in a kettle with 2 or 3 onions, 2 or 3 carrots cut in four parts, 2 celery stalks (also a bunch of hay); cover it with cold water, and as soon as it boils place the kettle on a corner of the range and let boil very slowly till tender (4 to 5 hours). 3d. Take the kettle from the range and let soak in the same water for about one hour. 4th. Take it out and let it cool; pare and trim the ham and serve entire for ball supper, picnics, etc.

NOTE.—The ham should be always cooked as indicated above, either to be served entire or in slices. It enters also into the preparation of a good many dishes, as ham and eggs, ham omelette, ham sandwiches, etc.; therefore we recommend to have some ready-cooked ham always in your ice-box.

302. JAMBON BRAISE AU MADERE.

BRAISED HAM WITH MADEIRA SAUCE. (*Releve.*)

PROPORTIONS.—For five persons:

Cooked ham as No. 301.	Madeira.................2 glassesful.
Stock ....2 glassesful.	*Time.*—1 hour.

PREPARATION.—1st. Cook the ham as indicated above, No. 301. 2d. Place it in a stove pan with 2 glassesful stock and 2 glassesful Madeira. 3d. Place a piece of buttered paper over the ham and let it bake in a warm oven (not too hot) for about one hour, while basting frequently*. 4th. Place the ham in a warm dish; pass the gravy through a strainer and serve with the gravy apart and mashed potatoes, spinage or sauer kraut apart. Carve as in the accompanying cut. The remainder of the ham may be utilized as indicated, No. 301.

303. JAMBON ROTI.

ROAST HAM. (*Roast.*)

PROPORTIONS.—For five persons:

Ham...............From 7 to 8 lbs.   Water.....................1 glassful.

Time.—$\begin{cases} \text{To freshen.........3 to 4 hours.} \\ \text{To roast............2 hours.} \end{cases}$

PREPARATION.—1st. Freshen a small ham of from 7 to 8 lbs. from 3 to 4 hours in cold water. 2d. Place it in a stove pan with 1 glassful water and let roast for about 2 hours, while basting and turning it from time to time. 3d. Prepare the gravy as indicated in No. 193, and serve with mashed potatoes or spinage.

304. JAMBON GRILLE.

BROILED HAM. (*Entree.*)†

PROPORTIONS.—For five persons:

Ham......................3 to 4 lbs.   *Time.*—10 minutes.

PREPARATION.—1st. Slice the ham about ¼ of an inch thick and broil on a bright fire until thoroughly cooked. 2d. Serve with mashed potatoes apart.

305. CARRE DE PORC ROTI.

ROAST PORK. (*Roast.*)

PROPORTIONS AND PREPARATION.—As for No. 193.

306. PETIT SALE AUX CHOUX.

BOILED SALTED PORK WITH CABBAGE. (*Entree.*)

PROPORTIONS.—For five persons:

Bacon, lean.............4 to 5 lbs.   Stock or water ..2 quarts.
Cabbage.................2 heads.   Salt and pepper. To suit the taste.

Time.—2½ hours.

---

* Remove the paper while basting.
† For breakfast and lunch only.

PREPARATION.—1st. Cut two cabbages in four parts (Savoy cabbages preferred because they are more tender). 2d. Boil in water for 10 minutes to remove the bitterness and drip. 3d. Place half of the cabbage in the kettle, add the bacon (washed and pared) cover with the remainder of the cabbage, add one quart of stock or water and let cook slowly for two hours. 4th. Skim off the floating grease, place the bacon in a hollow dish, drip the cabbage and place it on either side of the bacon.

NOTE.—Cook in this same way any part of salted pork. You may also add potatoes, carrots, etc., to the cabbages. This dish is especially advantageous in country towns during winter.

307. PETIT LARD GRILLE.

BROILED BACON. (*Entree.*)

PROPORTIONS.—For five persons:

Bacon..........................2 lbs.   *Time.*—10 minutes.

PREPARATION.—1st. Slice the bacon ¼ of an inch thick and let it broil on a bright fire or let it cook in a sauce pan till thoroughly cooked.

308. COTELETTES DE PORC GRILLEES. SAUCE TOMATE.

BROILED PORK WITH TOMATO SAUCE. (*Entree.*)

PROPORTIONS.—For five persons:

Pork chops........6 to 8.   Bread crumbs........3 tablespoonsful.
Melted butter......3 tablespoonsful.   *Time.*—20 minutes.

PREPARATION.—1st. Dip the chops in melted butter, roll them in bread crumbs and let them fry until well cooked. 2d. Serve with tomato sauce apart.

309. COTELETTES DE PORC. SAUCE ROBERT.

(*Entree.*)

PROPORTIONS AND PREPARATION.—As for No. 308, but serve with a Sauce Robert apart.

310. COTELETTES DE PORC A LA PARISIENNE.

PORK CHOPS A LA PARISIENNE. (*Entree.*)

PROPORTIONS.—For five persons:

Pork chops...........6 to 8.   Worcestershire s'ce.1 tablespoonful.
Butter ....2 tablespoonsful. Flour.....................1 tablespoonful.
White wine..........1 glassful.   Gherkins...............6.
Stock. ....¼ glassful.   *Time.*—1 hour.

PREPARATION.—1st. Fry the chops in a frying pan with two tablespoonsful butter till well colored, 2d. Place them in a dish and add in the same pan 1 tablespoonful flour, 1 glassful white wine, ⅓ glassful stock, 1 tablespoonful Worcestershire sauce, and 6 gherkins sliced. Boil a while and pour over the chops.

311. PIEDS DE COCHON GRILLES.

BROILED PIGS' FEET. (*Entree.*)*

PROPORTIONS.—For five persons:

Pigs' feet	6 to 8.	Thyme and laurel	A little.
Onions	2.		
Carrots	2.	Butter	4 to 5 tablespoonsful.
Celery	1 stalk.	Bread crumbs	3 to 4 tablespoonsful.

Time.— { To cook ....4 hours. { To broil.........10 to 15 minutes.

PREPARATION.—1st. Wash and clean the feet, place them in a kettle with two onions, two carrots, one celery stalk sliced, some thyme and laurel, cover with cold water and allow to cook till tender for about four hours. 2d. Cut the feet in 2, endwise, dip them in butter, roll in bread crumbs and let broil from 10 to 15 minutes. 3d. Serve with mustard and mashed potatoes.

312. PIEDS DE COCHON SAUCE VINAIGRETTE.

PIG'S FEET WITH VINAIGRETTE SAUCE. (*Entree.*)*

PROPORTIONS AND PREPARATION.—Cook the feet as indicated above, No. 311, cut them endwise and serve with a vinaigrette sauce, No. 165, apart.

313. SALADE DE PIEDS DE COCHON.

SALAD OF PIG'S FEET. (*Entree.*)*

PROPORTIONS:

Pig's feet	3.	Mustard	1 tablespoonful.
Oil	3 tablespoonsful.	Parsley	¼ handful.
Vinegar	4 tablespoonsful.	Ciboul	¼ handful.
	Salt and pepper	To suit the taste.	

PREPARATION.—1st. As 1st above, No. 311. 2d. Cut the feet in pieces about 2 inches long and put them in a salad dish where you have well mixed in advance 1 tablespoonful mustard, with 3 tablespoonsful oil, 4 tablespoonsful vinegar, ¼ handful chopped parsley, ¼ handful green ciboul, also chopped, salt and pepper to suit the taste. 3d. Mix well and serve for lunch or picnic party.

---

* For breakfast and lunch only.

SAUCES TO BE SERVED WITH MEATS.

314. SAUCE BEARNAISE.

BEARNAISE SAUCE. (*Yellow.*)

PROPORTIONS.

Vinegar..............¼ glassful.   Butter.........................¼ lb.
Echalotte............1.   Yolks ....3.
Time.—30 minutes.

PREPARATION.—1st. Place in a sauce pan ¼ glass white vinegar (teragon vinegar preferred) with 1 tablespoonful butter, 1 echalotte, a little pepper, and boil on bright fire till the vinegar is half boiled down. 2d. Place the sauce pan on a corner of the range, add while stirring a little butter and three eggs. 3d. Place the sauce pan in another larger one, half full of boiling water and add little by little, and while stirring about two tablespoonsful butter till the sauce is quite thick.

NOTE.—This sauce is one of the most palatable known, but it will require some practice.

315. SAUCE SOUBISE.

SOUBISE SAUCE. (*White.*)

PROPORTIONS.

Onions.........12.   Flour...........2 tablespoonsful.
Butter..........2 tablespoonsful.   Milk ....1 pint.
Time.—1 hour.

PREPARATION.—1st. Peel 12 fine onions, slice them and let them cook for 15 minutes in boiling water to remove their acrity. 2d. Drip them, dip them in cold water to cool them and drip them again carefully. 3d. Melt in a saucepan 2 tablespoonsful butter mixed with 2 tablespoonsful flour, add, while stirring, about 1 pint water and as soon as it boils add the onions and cook the whole slowly for about ½ hour. 4th. Sift through a sifter and serve apart with steaks, beaf steaks and chops.

316. SAUCE PARISIENNE.

(*White.*)

PROPORTIONS.

Echalottes.......2.   Flour...............⅛ tablespoonful.
Butter.............2 tablespoonsful.   Salt and pepper. To suit the taste.
Vinegar...........1 tablespoonful.   *Time.*—10 minutes.

PREPARATION.—Brown in a sauce pan 2 chopped echalottes with 1 tablespoonful butter, add 1 tablespoonful vinegar and 1 tablespoonful butter mixed with ⅛ tablespoonful flour. Boil awhile and pour over the steaks, beefsteaks or veal chops.

317. SAUCE BORDELAISE.

(Red.)

PROPORTIONS.—For five persons:

Echalottes......2.	Flour..............1 tablespoonful.
Butter...........1 tablespoonful.	Red wine.........1 glassful.
Vinegar.........1 tablespoonful.	*Time.*—10 to 15 minutes.

PREPARATION.—Brown in a sauce pan 2 chopped echalottes with 1 tablespoonful butter; add 1 tablespoonful vinegar; sprinkle over 1 tablespoonful flour; add 1 glassful red wine; let boil for 5 minutes; add a little chopped parsley and pour over the steaks.

318. SAUCE TOMATE.

TOMATO SAUCE. *(Red.)*

PROPORTIONS.—For five persons:

Tomatoes...........12.	Stock ....1 glassful.
Onions..............2.	Starch ....2 tablespoonful.
Carrots ....2.	Salt and pepper. To suit the taste.
Ham(cold boiled) 1 lb.	Cayenne pepper. A little.
Butter...............4 tablespoonsful.	*Time.*—1¼ hours.

PREPARATION.—1st. Slice 2 onions and 2 carrots quite fine; cut in dices about 1 lb. cold ham, if you have any cold (this is not indispensable, but gives very good taste); cook the whole for 5 minutes with 1 tablespoonful butter in quite a large sauce pan. 2d. Clean and slice 12 ripe tomatoes; add them in the sauce pan with 1 glassful stock, some thyme and laurel, some salt and pepper, and cook the whole for about 1 hour. 3d. Sift the whole through a sifter and place the pap obtained in another sauce pan with two tablespoonsful butter; warm, and when ready to serve add, while stirring, 2 tablespoonsful starch mixed with a little stock or water. Add a little cayenne pepper and serve apart.

319. SAUCE CREOLLE.

CREOLE SAUCE. *(Red.)*

PROPORTIONS.—For five persons:

Onions..............2.	Ham.................½ lb.
Garlic cloves... ..2.	Cayenne pepper. A little.
Butter..............2 tablespoonsful.	Salt and pepper. To suit the taste.
Tomatoes ....12.	*Time.*—1 hour.

PREPARATION.—1st. Chop 2 onions and 2 garlic cloves, which you brown for 5 minutes with 2 tablespoonsful butter. 2d. Add 12 tomatoes scalded in advance in boiling water and skinned; add also ½ lb. ham cut in dices, some salt and pepper; cook for 1 hour and pour over the steaks, beefsteaks or veal chops.

320. SAUCE POIVRADE.

PEPPER SAUCE. (*Brown.*)

PROPORTIONS.—For five persons:

Onion ....1.	Stock ....1 glassful.
Carrot............1.	Cayenne pepper. A little.
Flour.............1 tablespoonful.	Salt and pepper..To suit the taste.
Vinegar..........1 glassful.	*Time.*—¾ hour.

PREPARATION.—Melt in a sauce pan 1 tablespoonful butter, add 1 onion and 1 carrot, both chopped fine and cook for 5 minutes. 2d. Sprinkle over 1 tablespoonful flour, stir well and add 1 glassful vinegar, 1 glassful stock, some thyme and laurel, some salt and pepper, and cook slowly for ¼ hour. 3d. Sift the whole through a sifter, add a little cayenne pepper and serve apart or pour over the meat.

This sauce should be highly seasoned.

321. SAUCE PIQUANTE.

(*Brown.*)

PROPORTIONS AND PREPARATION.—As for the above, No. 321, but add 6 gerkins sliced quite fine.

322. SAUCE ROBERT.

(*Brown.*)

PROPORTIONS.—For five persons:

Onion ....1.	Parsley............½ handful.
Butter..........1 tablespoonful.	White wine.......1 glassful.
Flour...........1 tablespoonful.	Salt and pepper..To suit the taste.
Mustard........3 tablespoonsful.	*Time.*— ¼ hour.

PREPARATION.—Brown 1 chopped onion with 1 tablespoonful butter, sprinkle over 1 tablespoonful flour, add 3 tablespoonsful mustard, 1 glassful stock, some salt and pepper, some chopped parsley and boil the whole for ¼ hour.

323. SAUCE MENTHE.

MINT SAUCE. (*Green.*)

PROPORTIONS.—For five persons:

Mint leaves......1 handful.	Vinegar................½ glassful.
Sugar ....1 tablespoonful.	

PREPARATION.—Chop the mint leaves and mix them in a sauce boat with the vinegar and the sugar. Serve with the mutton leg.

GARNISHES TO BE SERVED WITH MEATS.

324. JARDINIERE.

GARNISH FOR A TENDERLOIN, A VEAL LOIN, OR SADDLE OF MUTTON.
PROPORTIONS.

Potatoes..................	} 1 cupful.	Small carrots.........	} 1 cupful.
Green peas..............		Cauliflowers carved	
Green beans............		Butter ....4 tablespoonsful.	

PREPARATION.—We call "jardiniere" a garnish made out of 2 or 4 potatoes fried in butter and several kinds of vegetables, as: green peas, green beans, small carrots, cauliflower cut in pieces of the size of a hazel-nut, etc , each of them having been cooked apart in some boiling water and then fried in butter. When the tenderloin, or loin, etc., is placed in a long dish, place a fried potato at each end and in the middle of the dish, then arrange the other vegetables with taste in small cakes around the meat.

325. RICHELIEU.

PROPORTIONS AND PREPARATION.—As for the above, No. 324, but add to the jardiniere 4 tomatoes and 4 mushrooms, stuffed.

326. FINANCIERE.

GARNISH FOR A TENDERLOIN, A VEAL LOIN OR A SADDLE OF MUTTON.
PROPORTIONS.

Mushrooms....... ....½ lb.	Fowl...............2 fillets.
Truffles ....¼ lb.	Flour ....1 tablespoonful.
Artichokes ....3.	

PREPARATION.—1st. Slice the mushrooms and the truffles, also the artichokes in quarters, cut the fillets of a fowl in small dices. 2d. Melt in a sauce pan 1 tablespoonful butter mixed with 1 tablespoonful flour, add through a strainer the gravy (No. 193) of the tenderloin, etc., add the mushrooms, the truffles and the artichokes, boil awhile and pour this sauce around the tenderloin, etc., placed in a long dish.

327. NAPOLITAINE.

GARNISH FOR A TENDERLOIN, VEAL LOIN OR A SADDLE OF MUTTON
PROPORTIONS.

Macaroni......1 lb.	Tomato catsup..2 tablespoonsful.
Butter.........4 tablespoonsful.	Mushrooms .....6.
Cheese..........¼ lb.	Ham...............¼ lb.

Time.—⅓ hour.

PREPARATION.—Do as indicated for the Macaroni a l'Italienne, add the mushrooms and the tomato catsup, and serve on both sides of the meat placed on a long dish.

328. NIVERNAISE.

GARNISH FOR A TENDERLOIN, VEAL LOIN, OR SADDLE OF MUTTON.
PROPORTIONS.

Small carrots..1 quart. Stock...... ....1 glassful.
Butter............4 tablespoonsful. *Time*—½ hour to 1 hour.

PREPARATION.—Pare and wash the carrots, place them in a sauce pan with 1 glassful stock, and 2 tablespoonsful butter and allow to cook till tender (from ½ to 1 hour). 2d. When ready to serve add 2 tablespoonsful butter.

329. FLAMANDE.

GARNISH FOR A BEEF ROUND OF ABOUT 12 LBS.
PROPORTIONS.

Cabbages.........................2. Saussage..............1 lb.
Carrots. ....3. Stock.................3 glassesful.
Bacon.............................1 lb. Salt and pepper....To suit the taste.
Time.—2¼ hours.

PREPARATION.—1st. As 1st and 2nd., No. 306, and add 3 carrots, cut in 4 to the cabbages and use 1 lb. bacon and 1 lb. sausages instead of 5 or 6 lbs. bacon. 2d. Pour over 3 glassesful stock and let cook slowly for about 2 hours. 3d. When ready to serve drip the cabbages and place them on both sides of the beef or serve them apart. In either case slice the bacon quite fine and place these slices and also the sausage on the cabbage. Serve with a horseradish sauce apart, No. 166.

330. BRETONNE.

GARNISH FOR A LEG OR SHOULDER OF MUTTON.
PROPORTIONS.

Kidney beans (white).......1 lb. Butter...............3 tablespoonsful.
Onion...............................1. Salt and pepper.To suit the taste.
Time.— { To soak......4 hours.
          { To cook......3¼ hours.

PREPARATION.—1st. Soak 1 lb. kidney beans in some cold water for about 4 hours, let them drip and cook in salted water till tender (for about 3 hours). 2d. When ready to serve chop 1 onion, let it brown in 1 tablespoonful butter, add the beans (dripped), stir well and add 2 tablespoonsful butter, sprinkle over some chopped parsley and serve apart with roast mutton.

RECAPITULATION.

BEEF.

ROASTS.

193. Rosbif a l'Anglaise.................Roast Beef.
195. Fillet Roti ....Roast Tenderloin.

RELEVES.

194. Cote de Boeuf Nivernaise ....Fore Ribs a la Nivernaise.
196. Fillet Braise Jardiniere ....Braised Tenderloin Jardiniere.
197.   "   "   Richelieu ....Braised Tenderloin Richelieu.
198.   "   "   Financiere...........Braised Tenderloin Financiere.
199.   "   "   Napolitaine .... "   "   Napolitaine.

ENTREES.

200. Entrecote Maitre d'Hotel........Broiled Steak a la Maitre d'Hotel.
201.   "   au Beurre D'Anchois.
202.   "   Soubise ....Broiled Steak a la Soubise.
203.   "   Bearnaise...............Broiled Steak with Bearnaise Sauce.
204.   "   Creole...................Broiled Steak with Creole Sauce.
205.   "   a la Parisienne ....Broiled Steak a la Parisienne.
206.   "   Bordelaise ....Broiled Steak Bordelaise.
207. Chataubriand, or Beefsteak } Beefsteak a la Maitre d'Hotel.
      Maitre d'Hotel................ }
208. Chataubriand, or Beefsteak au Beurre D'Anchois.
209.   "   "   Soubise.
210.   "   "   Bearnaise.
211.   "   "   Creole.
212.   "   "   Sauce Parisienne.
213.   "   "   Bordelaise.
214. Boeuf Saute a la Strogonoff......Beef Saute a la Strogonoff.
215. Fillet Saute aux Petits Pois .....Tenderloin with Green Peas.
216.   "   " aux Olives............Tenderloin Steak with Olives.
217.   "   " Bordelaise............Tenderloin Steak Bordelaise.
218.   "   " a l'Americaine ......Tenderloin Steak a l'Americaine.
219.   "   " aux Champignons.   "   "   with Mushrooms
220.   "   " aux Truffes..........   "   "   with Truffles.
221.   "   " a la Moelle...........   "   "   with Marrow.
222. Petits Fillets Rossini.
223. Bitocks a la Russe.
224. Stratzi a la Polonaise.
225. Boeuf a la Mode ....Beef a la Mode.
226. Culotte de Boeuf a la Flamande. Beef Round a la Flamande.
227.   "   " a l'Anglaise ... "   " a l'Anglaise.
228. Emince de Boeuf a la Bour- } Minced Boeuf a la Bourgeoise.
      geoise .... }
229. Boeuf en Miroton...................Beef with Onions.
230. Croquettes de Boeuf ....Beef Croquettes.
231. Boeuf Froid, Sauce Vinaigrette..Cold Beef with Sauce Vinaigrette.
232. Salade de Boeuf ....Beef Salad.

233. Beefsteak Pie.
234. Langue de Boef, Sauce Piquante. Tongue of Beef, Sauce Piquante.
235. Langue Froide........................Cold Salted or Smoked Tongue.
236. Sandwiches a la Langue ....Tongue Sandwiches.
237. Sandwich au Rosbif ....Beef Sandwich.
238. Cervelles de Boeuf a la Poulette. Beef Brain a la Poulette.
239. Cervelles au Beurre Noir.........Beef Brain with Brown Butter

VEAL.

ROAST.

240. Longe de Veau Rotie ....Roast Loin of Veal.

RELEVES.

241. Longe de Veau Jardiniere.......Loin of Veal Jardiniere.
242. Longe de Veau a la Creme......Loin of Veal with Cream.

ENTREES.

243. Veau a la Bourgeoise ....Veal a la Bourgeoise.
244. Poitrine de Veau Farcie ....Stuffed Veal Brisket.
245. Blanquette de Veau ....Blanquette of Veal.
246. Veau a la Provencale ....Veal a la Provencale.
247. Cotelette de Veau Grillee..........Broiled Veal Chop.
248.   "   "   aux Petits Pois Veal Chops with French Peas.
249.   "   "   Jardiniere......Veal Chops Jardiniere.
250.   "   "   aux Epinards. Veal Chops with Spinach.
251.   "   "   Sauce Tomate. Veal Chops with Tomato Sauce.
252.   "   "   aux Cham- } Veal Chops with Mushrooms.
     pignons .... }
253. Cotelette de Veau aux Truffes ...Veal Chops with Truffles.
254.   "   "   Milanaise......Veal Chops a la Milanaise.
255.   "   "   en Papilotte. Veal Chops in Papilottes.
256. Escaloppes de Veau Grillees } Escaloppes of Veal a la Maitre
     Maitre d'Hotel................ }   d'Hotel.
257. Escaloppes de Veau aux Pet- } Escaloppes of Veal with French Peas·
     its Pois......................... }
258. Escaloppes de Veau Jardiniere. Escaloppes of Veal Jardiniere.
259. Escaloppe de Veau aux Epi- } Escaloppe of Veal with Spinage.
     nards............................. }
260. Escaloppe de Veau, Sauce } Escaloppe of Veal with Tomato Sauce.
     Tomate. .... }
261. Foie de Veau Grille ....Broiled Veal Liver.
262.   "   "   aux Fines Herbes. Veal Liver Saute with Parsley.
263.   "   "   Saute au Madere.. Veal Liver Saute with Madeir
264.   "   "   Bonne Femme.....Backed Veal Liver.
265. Rognons de Veau Brochette.....Veal Kidney Broiled.
266. Rognons Saute au Madere ......Kidney Saute with Madeira.
267. Langue de Veau Sauce Piquante Veal Tongue with Sauce Piquante.
268. Riz de Veau a la Financiere....Sweet Breads a la Financiere.
269. "   "   aux Epinards..... Sweet Breads with Spinach.
270. Riz de Veau, Sauce Tomate ....Sweet Breads with Tomato Sauce.

271. Cervelles de Veau a la Poulette. Veal Brains a la Poulette.
272.   "   "   au Beurre Noir. Veal Brains with Browned Butter.
273. Tete de Veau Vinaigrette........Calf Head with Vinaigrette Sauce.
274. Tete de Veau Sauce Tomate.....Calf Head with Tomato Sauce.
275. Tete de Veau Sauce Piquante...Calf head with Sauce Piquante.
276. Pieds de Veau a la Poulette.....Calf Feet a la Poulette.
277.   "   "   Sauce Tomate...Calf Feet with Tomato Sauce.
278.   "   "   a la Vinaigrette. Calf Feet a la Vinaigrette.

MUTTON.

ROASTS.

279. Selle de Mouton a l'Anglaise ....Saddle of Mutton roasted.
286. Gigot D'Agneau Sauce Menthe.........Leg of Lamb with Mint Sauce.
287. Epaule de Mouton a la BonneFemme..Mutton Shoulder a la.
288.   "   "   Farcie.............Stuffed Mutton Shoulder.

RELEVES.

280. Selle de Mouton Jardiniere...............Saddle of Mutton Jardiniere.
281.   "   "   Richelieu.................   "   "   Richelieu.
282. Gigot de Mouton a la Francaise........Leg of Mutton a la Francaise.

ENTREES.

283. Gigot de Mouton a la Bretonne..........Leg of Mutton ala Bretonne.
284.   "   "   Bouilli a l'Anglaise.....Boiled leg of Mutton.
285.   "   "   "   Sauce aux } Boiled l eg of Mutton, Caper
     Capres............................ .... }   sauce.
289. Blanquette D'Agneau........................Blanquette of Lamb.
290. Ragout de Mouton.............................French Mutton Stew.
291.   "   "   a l'Irlandaise............Irish stew.
292. Cotelettes de Mouton Grillees a la }
     Francaise...................... ....} Broiled French mutton chops.
293. Cotelettes de Mouton Panees...........{ Mutton chops with bread
                                 crumbs.
204.   "   "   a l'Anglaise......English mutton chops.
295. Shachlick de Mouton a la Circas- } Brochettes of mutton a la Cir-
     sienne..................................... }   cassienne.
206. Rognons de Mouton Brochette...........Broiled Mutton Kidney.
297.   "   "   Saute au Madere. } Mutton Kidneys saute with
                                 Madeira.
298. Cervelle de Mouton Poulette.............Mutton Brains a la Poulette.
299.   "   "   at Beurre Noir... { Mutton Brains with browned
                                 butter.
300. Pieds de Mouton Poulette.................Mutton feet a la Poulette.

PORK.

RELEVES.

301. Jambon Froid...............................Cold Ham.
302. Jambon Braise au Madere................ { Braised Ham with Madeira
                                 sauce.

ROASTS.

303. Jambon Roti.................................Roast Ham.
305. Carre de Porc Roti..........................Roast Pork.

ENTREES.

304. Jambon Grille...............................Broiled Ham
306. Petit Sale aux Choux..................... } Boiled Salted Pork with Cabbage.
307. Petit Lard Grille...........................Broiled Bacon.
308. Cotelettes de Porc Grilles, Sauce Tomate.. } Broiled Pork with Tomato Sauce.
309. Cotelettes de Porc Grilles, Sauce Robert....................................... } Broiled Pork with Robert Sauce.
310. Cotelettes de Porc Grilles, a la Parisienne.................................... } Pork Chops a la Parisienne.
311. Pieds de Cochon Grilles.....................Broiled Pig's Feet.
312. Pieds de Cochon, Sauce Vinaigrette. } Pig's Feet with Vinaigrette Sauce.
313. Salade de Pieds de Cochon...............Salad of Pig's Feet.
176. Oeufs au Jambon............................Ham and eggs.
186. Omelette au Jambon........................Omelet with Ham.
177. Oeuf au Lard...............................Eggs and Bacon.
187. Omelette au Lard...........................Omelet with Bacon.

SAUCES TO BE SERVED WITH MEAT.

161. Maitre d'Hotei.......................White and green.
201. Beurre d'Anchois.....................Light brown.
314. Sauce Bearnaise.....................Bearnaise Sauce. Yellow.
315. Sauce Soubise........................Soubise Sauce. White.
316. Sauce Parisienne.....................White.
317. Sauce Bordelaise.....................Red.
118. Sauce Tomatte.......................Tomato Sauce. Red.
319. Sauce Creolle.......................Creole Sauce. Red.
320. Sauce Poivrade.......................Pepper Sauce. Brown.
321. Sauce Piquante.......................Brown.
322. Sauce Robert.........................Brown.
165. Sauce Vinaigrette....................
323. Sauce Menthe.........................Mint Sauce. Green.
166. Sauce Raifort.......................Horseradish Sauce. White.

GARNISHES TO BE SERVED WITH MEAT.

324. Jardiniere................................
325. Richelieu................................
326. Financiere...............................
327. Napolitaine..............................
328. Nivernaise...............................
329. Flamende................................
330. Bretonne..................................
358. Petits Pois a la Francaise.........French Peas.
361. Haricots Verts a l'Anglaise.......Green Beans with Butter.

380. Tomattes Farcies................Stuffed Tomatoes.
384. Mais au Beurre.....................Sweet Corn with Butter.
395. Puree de Pommes de Terre.......Mashed Potatoes.
397. Croquettes de Pommes de Terre..Potato Croquettes.
396. Pommes de Terre Duchesse......
393. Pommes de Terre a la Creme....Potatoes with Cream.
400. Pommes de Terre Frittes.........Fried Potatoes.
392. Pommes de Terre Sautees........Potatoes Fried in Butter.
399. Pommes de Terre Farcies.........Stuffed Potatoes.
409. Croquettes de Oatmeal............Oatmeal Croquettes.
405. Riz a la Milanaise..................Rice a la Milanaise.
407. Riz a la Creole.....................Rice a la Creole.
406. Riz a la Georgienne.................Rice a la Georgienne..
378. Choucroute a la Strasbourgeoise.Saurkrout a la Strasbourgeoise.

POULTRY.

331. GENERAL REMARKS.

1st. As a rule select young fowls for roasting. The older ones should be served only in fricassee or boiled. 2d. Remove the feathers carefully with the hand and not by first scalding in boiling water. Clean and wash carefully the inside; singe with a burning newspaper placed on the top of the stove; and tie the legs and the wings to the body before roasting.

TURKEY.

332. DINDE ROTIE.

ROAST TURKEY. (*Roast.*)

PROPORTIONS.—For five persons:
Turkey...........6 to 7 lbs.   Water..........1 glassful.
Butter..3 tablespoonsful.   *Time.*—1½ hours.

PREPARATION.—1st. Prepare the turkey as indicated No. 331. 2d. Place the turkey in a stove pan. Rub it over with about three tablespoonsful butter; add 1 glassful water and roast from 1½ to 2 hours according to the size as indicated No. 193, make the gravy as indicated No. 193, and serve it apart.

NOTE.—For a family dinner the fillets will be sufficient. Serve the legs and the body cold for breakfast, with a sauce Remoulade, No. 164.

333. ABATIS DE DINDE.

TURKEY GIBLETS. (*Entree.*)*

PROPORTIONS.—For five persons:

Giblets........Wings, feet, neck, gizzard, liver.	Stock ....1 glassful.
	Small onions .....12.
Bacon..........1 lb.	Carrots.............3.
Butter..........2 tablespoonsful.	Parsley ....½ handful.
Flour...........2 tablespoonsful.	Salt and pepper..To suit the taste.
Water..........1 glassful.	*Time.*—1¼ hours.

PREPARATION.—1st. When preparing the turkey for roasting, put aside the giblets (the wings, feet, gizzard, liver, etc.). They will constitute a very good family dish. 2d. Brown the giblets in a sauce pan with 1 lb. bacon cut in dices and 2 tablespoonsful butter. 3d. Sprinkle over 1 tablespoonful flour, add 1 glassful water and 1 glassful stock or 1 pint of water, some salt and pepper, ¼ handful parsley (tied), 12 small onions, 3 carrots cut in four endwise and in thirds crosswise. Cook slowly for 1¼ hours. Skim off the floating grease and serve in a hollow dish.

CHICKEN.

334. POULET ROTI.

ROAST CHICKEN. (*Roast.*)

PROPORTIONS.—For five persons:

Chickens......2.	Water...................1 glassful.
Butter..........2 tablespoonsful.	*Time.*—¾ hour.

PREPARATION.—Do as indicated for the roast turkey No. 332, but roast only for about ¾ of an hour.

335. POULET GRILLE.

BROILED CHICKEN. (*Entree.*)†

PROPORTIONS.—For five persons:

Young chickens.................2.   Butter...........4 tablespoonsful.
Time.—50 minutes.

PREPARATION.—1st. Prepare the chickens as indicated No. 331, cut them in two endwise, dip them in melted butter and broil on bright fire on both sides until thoroughly cooked.

---

* For breakfast only.
† For breakfast or lunch.

336. COTELETTES DE VOLAILLE.

FOWL CUTLETS.   (*Entree* or Hors d'Œuvre.)*

PROPORTIONS.—For five persons:

Chickens............................ 3. Butter............¼ lb.
Eggs......................... .... 2. Bread crumbs..4 tablespoonsful.
Time.—20 minutes.

PREPARATION.—1st.   Take off the fillets, keeping with them the end of the wing bone.   Dip them in beaten egg, roll in bread crumbs and fry in butter in a shallow stew pan.   2d.   Serve in a warm dish and pour over the butter in which they have been fried.

NOTE.—Use the body in the stock soup No. 1.

337. FILLETS DE VOLAILLE.

FILLETS OF FOWL.   (*Hors d'Œuvre.*)*   See No. 56.

338. FRITTO DE POULET A L'ITALIENNE.

FRIED CHICKEN.   (*Entree.*)†

PROPORTIONS.—For five persons:

Young chickens...2.   Lemon................1.
Milk..................1 pint.   Salt and pepper...To suit the taste.
Flour..................3 tablespoonsful. Fat or lard.........Enough to fry.
Parsley...............1 handful.   *Time.*—¼ hour.

PREPARATION.—1st.   Cut each chicken in about 8 pieces, sprinkle with salt and pepper, dip the pieces in milk, roll them in flour and fry in fat or lard till well colored.   Serve on a folded napkin with parsley fried in the same fat and a lemon cut in 5.

339. CROQUETTES DE VOLAILLE.

CROQUETTES OF FOWL.   (*Hors d'Œuvre.*)* Same as No. 55.

340. POULE AU RIZ.

BOILED CHICKEN WITH RICE.   (*Entree.*)

PROPORTIONS.—For five persons:

Hen.................................1. Hollandaise sauce.......No. 151.
Riz a la Georgienne.

PREPARATION.—1st.   Boil the hen as indicated in the stock soup No. 1, and serve with a Hollandaise sauce No. 151, and rice a la Georgienne, apart.

---

* For select lunch or ball supper.
† For breakfast or lunch.

341. JEUNE POULET SAUTE FERMIERE.

YOUNG CHICKEN SAUTE A LA FERMIERE. (*Entree.*)*

PROPORTIONS.—For five persons:

Chickens...............................2.   Parsley...............¼ handful.
Butter..............................¼ lb.   Salt and pepper.....To suit the taste.
Onion....................................1.   *Time.*—30 minutes

PREPARATION.—1st. Prepare the chicken as indicated No. 331, 2d; take off the legs and cut them in two; take off the wings, but not the fillets, and cut the body in five pieces.† 2d. Warm in a shallow stew pan ¼ lb. butter, add one chopped onion, brown a while and add the chicken, sprinkle over some salt and pepper and fry on bright fire from 15 to 20 minutes. 3d. Sprinkle over some chopped parsley and serve hot.

342. POULET SAUTE MARENGO.

(*Entree.*)

PROPORTIONS.—For five persons:

Chickens............2.   Tomato catsup.....4 tablespoonsful.
Olive oil.............3 tablespoonsful.   Flour...................1 tablespoonful.
Onion.................1.   Parsley................¼ handful.
Garlic clove........1.   Salt and pepper....To suit the taste.
White wine.........½ glassful.   *Time.*—20 to 30 minutes.

PREPARATION.—1st. As 1st. and 2d, No. 341. 2d. Warm in a shallow stew pan 3 tablespoonsful olive oil. Add 1 chopped onion, 1 chopped garlic clove, brown awhile, add the chicken and fry till well colored. 3d. Sprinkle over 1 tablespoonful flour, add ½ glassful white wine, 4 tablespoonsful tomato catsup, boil for five minutes. 4th. Sprinkle over some chopped parsley and serve in a hollow dish with some toast fried in butter.

343. POULET SAUTE AUX CHAMPIGNON.

CHICKEN SAUTE WITH MUSHROOMS. (*Entree.*)

PROPORTIONS.—For five persons:

Chickens........2   Flour..............1 tablespoonful.
Mushrooms....½ lb. can.   White wine......1 glassful.
Onion...........1.   Stock..............1 glassful.
Butter............3 tablespoonsful. Salt and pepper.To suit the taste.
Time.—20 to 30 minutes.

---

* For breakfast or lunch.

† Cut the body in two endwise between the back and the breast, then each half in two crosswise, and again the breast in two endwise. (See cut.)

PREPARATION.— 1st. and 2d. as No. 342, but do not use the garlic clove and fry the chicken in butter instead of oil. 3d. Sprinkle over 1 tablespoonful flour, add 1 glassful white wine, 1 glassful stock, ½ lb. can mushrooms sliced, some salt and pepper, cook for five minutes and serve in a hollow, warm dish.

344. POULET SAUTE A LA HONGROISE.

CHICKEN SAUTE A LA HONGROISE. (*Entree.*)

PROPORTIONS. — For five persons:

Chickens............2.		Worcestershire sauce.1 tablespoonful.	
Butter................3 tablespoonsful.		Paprica or cayenne	
Young onions.....6.		pepper..............A little.	
Parsley..............½ handful.		Salt and pepper........To suit the taste.	
Cream................1 glassful.		*Time.*—½ hour.	

PREPARATION.—1st. As for No. 342. 2d. Melt in a sauce pan 3 tablespoonsful butter, add the chicken cut in pieces, 6 young onions (the green part and the bulb), cut in four lengthwise and in three or four crosswise, ½ handful parsley, cook slowly for about 15 minutes while turning the chicken from time to time. 3d. Add 1 glassful cream, 1 tablespoonful Worcestershire sauce, a little paprica or cayenne pepper and serve in a hollow dish with rice a la Georgienne, apart.

345. FRICASSEE DE POULET.

FRICASSEE OF CHICKEN. (*Entree.*)

PROPORTIONS.—For five persons:

Chickens or hens......2.	Flour............1 tablespoonful.
Onions.....................2.	Butter..........2 tablespoonsful.
Carrots....................2.	Milk.............2 tablespoonsful.
Parsley....................½ handful.	Yolks............2.

Time. — { To freshen, ¼ hour. / To cook, 1 to 2 hours. }

PREPARATION.—1st. As for No. 342. 2d. Soak the chicken in cold water for about ¼ hour. 3d. Place it in a shallow stew pan with 2 onions sliced, 2 carrots cut in four, ½ handful parsley (tied), cover with water and allow to cook slowly till tender (from 1 to 2 hours). 4th. Drip the chickens and place them in a sauce pan in which you have melted 2 tablespoonsful butter mixed with 2 tablespoonsful flour. Stir well and add through a strainer the stock in which the chickens have been boiled. 5th. When ready to serve place the sauce pan on a corner of the range and add two yolks beaten with two tablespoonsful milk. Serve in a hollow dish with rice a la Georgienne, apart.

GUINEA HENS.

346. PINTADE ROTIE.

ROAST GUINEA HEN. (*Roast.*)

PROPORTIONS AND PREPARATION.—As for the roast chicken, but one Pintado hen will be sufficient for five.

347. PINTADO BRAISEE.

BRAISED GUINEA HEN.

PROPORTIONS.—For five persons:

Pintado	1.	Carrot	1.
Stock	1 glassful.	Thyme and laurel	A little.
Onion	1.	Salt and pepper	To suit the taste.

Time.—1⅓ hours.

PREPARATION.—1st. Clean the pintado as indicated No. 331, 2d. 2d. Place it in a stew pan with 1 onion and 1 carrot sliced, some thyme and laurel, 1 glassful stock, cover the sauce pan and cook slowly for 1⅓ hours.

GOOSE.

348. OIE ROTI.

ROAST GOOSE. (*Roast.*)

PROPORTIONS.—For five persons:

Goose	5 to 6 lbs.	Water	1 glassful.
Butter	2 tablespoonsful.	*Time.*—1⅓ to 2 hours.	

PREPARATION.—1st. Prepare the goose as indicated, No. 331. 2d. Rub it with 2 tablespoonsful butter, place it in a stove pan, add 1 glassful water, and roast from 1⅓ to 2 hours as indicated, No. 193. 3d. Skim off the floating grease* and serve with the gravy (No. 193) apart.

349. ABATIS D'OIE.

GOOSE GIBLETS. (*Entree.*)†

PROPORTIONS AND PREPARATION.—As for No. 333.

DUCKS.

350. CANARD ROTI.

ROAST DUCK. (*Roast.*)

PROPORTIONS.—For five persons:

Young ducks	2.	Toast	2.
Butter	4 tablespoonsful.	*Time.*—1⅓ to 2 hours.	

---

* The grease of geese is very palatable, especially for fried potatoes, etc.
† For breakfast only.

PREPARATION.—1st. Prepare the ducks as indicated, No. 331. 2d. Rub them with 2 tablespoonsful butter, place in a stove pan and roast as indicated for the roast chicken, No. 334. Serve on toast made as follows: Fry the toast in butter, spread over the liver chopped with some salt and pepper and 1 tablespoonful butter, and warm in an oven for 5 minutes before serving the duck.

351. CANARD AUX PETITS POIS.

DUCK WITH FRENCH PEAS. (*Entree.*)

PROPORTIONS.—For five persons:

Ducks	2.	Stock	1 glassful.
Butter	3 tablespoonsful.	Peas	1 quart.
Bacon	½ lb.	Salt and pepper	To suit the taste
Flour	1 tablespoonful.	*Time.*—1¼ hours.	

PREPARATION.—Warm in a stew pan 3 tablespoonsful butter, add the ducks (prepared as indicated No. 331), and let them brown till well colored. 2d. Add ½ lb. bacon cut in dices, sprinkle over 1 tablespoonful flour, add 1 glassful stock, 1 quart green peas, ½ handful parsley (tied), some salt and pepper and cook for about 1 hour. Serve the ducks and the peas apart, as it will be easier to carve.

352. CANARD AUX NAVETS.

DUCK WITH TURNIPS. (*Entree.*)

PROPORTIONS AND PREPARATION.—As for the above, No. 351, but instead of peas add 6 or 8 turnips, cut in 6 or 8 according to their size, and fried awhile in two tablespoonsful butter and 1 tablespoonful sugar.

353. CANARD AUX OLIVES.

DUCK WITH OLIVES. (*Entree.*)

PROPORTIONS AND PREPARATION.—As for No. 351, but instead of peas add 2 dozen olives stoned about 10 minutes before serving.

354. CANARD AUX ONIONS.

DUCK WITH SMALL ONIONS. (*Entree.*)

As for the above, No. 351, but instead of peas add 24 small onions (raw).

PIGEONS.

355. PIGEONS ROTIS.

ROAST PIGEONS. (*Roast.*)

PROPORTIONS.—For five persons:

Pigeons	5.	Bacon	¼ lb.
	Toasts	5.	

PREPARATION. 1st. Prepare the pigeons as indicated No. 331, but the flesh of pigeon being quite lean tie over it 1 thin slice of fat bacon (leaf lard) and roast as indicated from 20 to 30 minutes. 2d. Serve on toast fried in butter and allow one pigeon to each guest.

356. PIGEONS A LA CRAPAUDINE.

BROILED PIGEONS. (*Entree.*)

PROPORTIONS.—For five persons:

Pigeons........................3. Bread crumbs..6 tablespoonsful.
Butter ....¼ lb. Parsley...........½ handful.
Time.—50 minutes.

PREPARATION.—1st. Prepare as indicated No. 331. 2d. Cut the pigeon in two endwise, flatten with a cleaver, dip in melted butter, roll in bread crumbs and fry on a not too bright fire and serve with a Maitre d'Hotel (No. 161) apart, in which you have added the juice of ¼ of a lemon. Serve with a lemon cut in 6 pieces.

357. PIGEON AUX PETITS POIS.

PIGEON WITH FRENCH PEAS.

PROPORTIONS AND PREPARATION.—As for the duck with French peas, No. 351.

RECAPITULATION.

331. General Remarks.

TURKEY.

332. Dinde Rotie....................Roast Turkey. (Roast.)
333. Abatis de Dinde.....................Turkey Giblets.   (Entree.)

CHICKEN.

334. Poulet Roti...... ....Roast Chicken. (Roast.)
335. Poulet Grille......................…...Broiled Chicken.   (Entree.)
336. Cotelettes de Volaille...........… ..Fowl Cutlets. (Entree.)
337. Fillets de Volaille ....…....Fillets of Fowl. (Hors d'Œuvre.)
338. Fritto de Poulet a l'Italienne.....Fried Chicken. (Entree.)
339. Croquettes de Volaille ....Croquettes of Fowl. (Hors d'Œuvre.
340. Poule au riz......………... ....Boiled Chicken, with Rice. (Entree.)
341. Jeune Poulet Saute Fermiere { Chicken Saute a la Fermiere. (Entree.)
342. Poulet Saute Marengo. (Entree.)
343. Poulet Saute aux Chámpignon { Chicken Saute, with Mushrooms. (Entree.)
344. Poulet Saute a la Hongroise.. { Chicken Saute a la Hongroise. (Entree.)
345. Fricassee de Poulet ....Fricassee of Chicken. (Entree.)

GUINEA HENS.

346. Pintade Rotie ....…...Roast Guinea Hen. (Roast.)
347. Pintade Braisee.......................Braised Guinea Hen.   (Entree.)

GOOSE.

348. Oie Roti...... ....Roast Goose. (Roast.)
349. Abatis d'Oie.............................Goose Giblets. (Entree.)

DUCKS.

350. Canard Roti.........................Roast Duck. (Roast.)
351. Canard aux Petits Pois............Duck with French Peas. (Entree.)
352. Canard aux Navets ....Duck with Turnips. (Entree.)
353. Canard aux Olives ....Duck with Olives. (Entree.)
354. Canard aux Onions.. ....Duck with Small Onions. (Entree.)

PIGEONS.

355. Pigeons Rotis ....Roast Pigeons. (Roast.)
356. Pigeons a la Crapaudine...........Broiled Pigeons.   (Entree.)
337. Pigeon aux Petits Pois ....Pigeon with French Peas.

GAME.

VENISON.

357 a SELLE DE CHEVREUIL ROTIE.

SADDLE OF ROASTED VENISON. (*Roast.*)

PROPORTIONS. — For ten persons:

Saddle of venison......12 to 14 lbs.
Bacon.....................1 lb.
Water.....................1 glassful.
Time. { To pickle..24 to 36 hours.
        { To cook...1½ hours.

PREPARATIONS.—1st. Pare the saddle and trim off the grease. Lard it with about 1 lb. bacon cut in small strips. 2d. Place the meat in a dish longer than the saddle and hollow, and pour over it a pickling made as indicated No. 357 z, No. 1. 3d. Pickle from 24 to 38 hours, taking care to baste from time to time. 4th. Drip the saddle and roast it as indicated for the saddle of mutton No. 279. Serve with potato croquettes No. 397 around the dish and the gravy (No. 193) apart.

357b. SELLE DE CHEVREUIL. SAUCE POIVRADE.

SADDLE OF VENISON, WITH SAUCE POIVRADE. (*Releve.*)

PROPORTIONS AND PREPARATION.—As for No. 357 a, and serve with a sauce poivrade, No. 357x, in which you have poured the gravy of the saddle after having carefully skimmed all the floating grease.

357c. SELLE DE CHEVREUIL. SAUCE VENAISON.

SADDLE OF VENISON. VENISON SAUCE. (*Releve.*)

PROPORTIONS AND PREPARATION.—As for No. 357a, and serve with a sauce venison, No. 357y apart.

357d. CUISSOT DE CHEVREUIL ROTI.

ROAST LEG OF VENISON. (*Roast.*)

PROPORTIONS AND PREPARATION.—As for No. 357a.

357e. CUISSOT DE CHEVREUIL. SAUCE POIVRADE.

LEG OF VENISON. SAUCE POIVRADE. (*Releve.*)

PROPORTIONS AND PREPARATION.—As for No. 357c.

357f. CUISSOT DE CHEVREUIL. SAUCE VENAISON.

PROPORTIONS AND PREPARATION.—As for No. 357c. (*Releve.*)

357g. FILLET DE CHEVREUIL. SAUCE VENAISON.

VENISON STEAK. VENISON SAUCE. (*Entree*).

PROPORTIONS.—For five persons:

Venison tenderloin.........3 lbs.   Butter..........3 tablespoonsful.

Time.—15 to 20 minutes.

PREPARATION.—1st. Pickle the tenderloin as indicated No. 357a. Cook it as indicated for the Fillet Saute No. 215, and serve with venison sauce apart, No. 357y.

357h. COTELETTES DE CHEVREUIL. SAUCE POIVRADE.

VENISON CHOPS OR CUTLETS. SAUCE POIVRADE. (*Entree.*)

PROPORTIONS.—For five persons:

Venison chops.......5 to 6.   Butter...................3 tablespoonsful
Salt and pepper....To suit the taste.   *Time.*—15 minutes.

PREPARATIONS.—1st.—Pickle the chops for 24 hours in the pickling No. 357z, No. 1 (but only ¼ of the proportion indicated.) Fry in butter for about 15 minutes. Serve with sauce poivrade, No. 357x apart.

357i. CIVET DE CHEVREUIL.

VENISON STEW. (*Entree.*)

PROPORTIONS.—For five persons:

Venison brisket..........   Stock ....1 glassful.
  or shoulder........7 to 8 lbs.   Salt and pepper...To suit the taste.
Butter.................3 tablespoonsful.   Small onions ......20.
Flour.................2 tablespoonsful.   Parsley.............⅛ handful.
Red wine.............1 glassful.   *Time.*—1¾ hours.

PREPARATION.—1st. Cut the brisket or shoulder (which are too tough to be roasted) in pieces about ½ the size of the hand. 2d. Warm in a stew pan 3 tablespoonsful butter, add the buck and let brown a while.

3d. Sprinkle over 1 tablespoonful flour, add 1 glassful stock, 1 glassful red wine, some salt and pepper, 1 handful parsley (tied), boil a while and add about 20 small onions and let cook slowly for 1½ hours. 4th. Skim off the floating grease and serve in a hollow. warm dish.

HARE.

357j. RABLE DE LIEVRE.

ROAST BACK OF HARE. (*Roast.*)

PROPORTIONS.—For five persons:

Hare..1.
Bacon..¼ lb.
Pickling......................................No. 421.
Time.— { To pickle...3 to 4 hours
           { To roast.....1 hour.

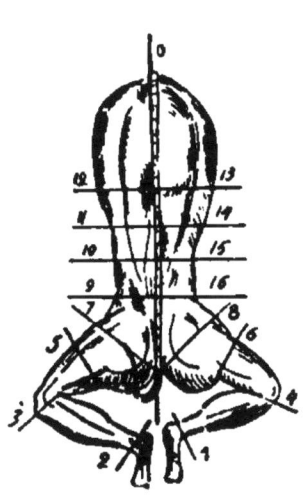

PREPARATION.—1st. Skin and clean the back of a hare. Let it pickle for about 3 hours in pickling, No. 421. 2d. Place it in a stove pan as indicated by the accompanying cut with glassful of the pickling and the vegetables of the same. Sprinkle over some salt and pepper and roast as indicated, No. 193, for about 1 hour. Serve the gravy (No. 193) apart.

357k. CIVET DE LIEVRE A LA PARISIENNE.

STEW OF HARE A LA PARISIENNE. (*Entree.*)

PROPORTIONS.—For five persons:

Hare ....1.   Flour ....2 tablespoonsful.
Bacon............½ lb.   Red wine.......1 glassful.
Small onions.24.   Stock ....1 glassful.
Butter...........2 tablespoonsful.   Vinegar.........¼ glassful.
Time.—1¾ hours.

PREPARATION.—1st. Skin and wash the hare, cut it in pieces about the size of an egg. 2d. Melt in a sauce pan 2 tablespoonsful butter. Fry ¼ lb. bacon cut in dices, about 1½ inches long and ⅛ inch thick. Add about 24 small onions, brown the whole till well colored, then take the onions and bacon out of the butter and place them aside. 3d. Place the hare in a saucepan. Fry and sprinkle over 2 tablespoonsful flour, stir well the whole and add 1 glassful red wine and 1 glassful stock, some salt and pepper, and boil awhile. 4th. Add the onions and the bacon (already half cooked) and cook slowly for about 1½ hours. 5th. When ready to serve mix the liver (the gall bladder having been removed) with ¼ glass vinegar and pour it in the sauce pan.   Serve in a hollow warm dish.

RABBIT.

357l. RABLE DE LAPIN.

Roast Back of Rabbit.   (*Roast.*)

Proportions and Preparation.—As No. 357j.

357m. CIVET DE LAPIN.

Rabbit Stew, No. 1.   (*Entree.*)

Proportions and Preparation.—As No. 357k.

357n. GIBELOTTE DE LAPIN.

Rabbit Stew, No. 2.   (*Entree.*)

Proportions and Preparation.—As for No. 357k but use white instead of red wine.

357o. LAPIN SAUTE CHASSEUR.

Rabbit Saute a la Chasseur.   (*Entree.*)

Proportions.—For five persons:

Rabbit ....1.	Parsley.................¼ handful.
Butter.... ....3 tablespoonsful.	Lemon...................½.
Onions ....2.	*Time.*—50 minutes.

Preparation.—1st. Skin and clean the rabbit and cut it in pieces the size of an egg.   2d. Melt in a sauce pan 3 tablespoonsful butter, add the rabbit, add 2 onions chopped, ¼ handful parsley chopped, sprinkle over some salt and pepper and let cook for about 50 minutes (covered).   Add the juice of ½ lemon and serve for breakfast or lunch.

WILD TURKEY.

357p. DINDE SAUVAGE ROTIE.

Wild Turkey Roasted.   (*Roast.*)

Proportions and Preparation.—As for the roast turkey No. 832.

357q. SALMIS DE DINDE.

SALMIS OF TURKEY. (*Entree.*)

PROPORTIONS.—For five persons:

Turkey.........The body of one.	Flour................2 tablespoonsful.
Onion...........1.	Madeira...... ......2 glassesful.
Butter...........2 tablespoonsful.	Stock................2 glassesful.

Time.—1½ hour.

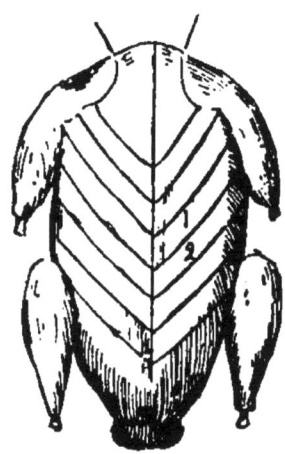

PREPARATION.—1st. Carve the body of a turkey which you have already served roasted and place the flesh aside. 2d. Melt in a sauce pan 2 table-spoonsful butter, add 1 chopped onion, fry a while, sprinkle over 2 tablespoonsful flour, add 2 glassesful madeira and 2 glassesful stock, let boil a while, add the bones and the paring of the turkey broken fine in a mortar, and cook the whole for about 1 hour. 3d. Pass this sauce through a sifter and pour over the turkey which you have placed in another sauce pan. Warm the whole for about five minutes and serve in a hollow dish.

PRAIRIE CHICKEN, PHEASANT, PARTRIDGE.

357r. POULE DE PRAIRIE, PERDRIX OU FAISANT ROTI.

PRAIRIE CHICKEN, PHEASANT OR PARTRIDGE. (*Roast.*)

PROPORTIONS AND PREPARATION.—As for roasted guinea hen, No. 383, but roast on a bright fire.

357s. POULE DE PRAIRIE, PERDRIX OU FAISANT GRILLE.

PRAIRIE CHICKEN, PHEASANT OR PARTRIDGE BROILED. (*Entree.*)

PROPORTIONS AND PREPARATION.—As for the pigeons a la craupau-dine, No. 356.

357t. SALMIS DE POULE DE PRAIRIE, DE FAISANT OU DE PERDRIX.

SALMIS OF PRAIRIE CHICKEN, PHEASANT OR PARTRIDGE. (*Entree.*)

Roast two pheasants, prairie chickens or partridge as indicated No. 357r and as indicated for the salmis of turkey, No. 357q.

357u. CANARD SAUVAGE ROTI.

WILD DUCK ROASTED. (*Roast.*)

PROPORTIONS AND PREPARATION.—As for the roasted duck No. 350 but roast on bright fire.

357v. SALMIS DE CANARD SAUVAGE.

SALMIS OF WILD DUCK. (*Entree.*)

Do as indicated, No. 357q.

357w. SMALL BIRDS.

(QUAIL, SNIPE, REED BIRDS, ETC.) (*Roast.*)

The small birds as quail, reed birds, snipe, etc., are roasted in a stew pan with butter or with some bacon cut in dices. They should be cooked on a bright fire to be very tender and served on toast fried in butter with their own gravy.

SAUCES TO BE SERVED WITH THE GAME.

357x. SAUCE POIVRADE.
See No. 320.

357y. SAUCE VENAISON

VENISON SAUCE. (*Brown.*)

PROPORTIONS.

Butter............2 tablespoonsful.	Pickling No. 357z...1 glassful and
Flour..........2 tablespoonsful.	its vegetables.
Stock............2 glassesful.	Thyme and laurel..To suit the taste.
Pepper..........To suit the taste.	*Time.*—1 hour.

PREPARATION.—Melt in a sauce pan 2 tablespoonsful butter mixed with 2 tablespoonsful flour, and add, while stirring, 2 glassesful stock, 1 glass of the pickling No. 357z, No. 1, with its vegetables, some fresh thyme and laurel, some pepper; let cook slowly for an hour and when ready to serve, sift the whole through a sifter or strainer.

357z. PICKLING.

No. 1.　PROPORTION.—For a saddle or a leg of venison:

Butter............2 tablespoonsful.	Thyme and laurel .....A little.
Onions..........2.	Whole pepper............Some.
Carrots :........2.	Vinegar....................1 quart.
Water.....................1 quart.	

PREPARATIONS.—1st. Melt in a sauce pan 2 tablespoonsful butter, add 2 onions and 2 carrots sliced fine, some thyme and laurel, some whole pepper, boil a while, add 1 quart water and 1 quart vinegar, let boil again for five minutes and cool.

No. 2.—PROPORTIONS.—For 1 hare or 1 rabbit:

Onion....................................1.   Parsley....................½ handful.
White wine............... ....2 glassesful.

PREPARATION.—Slice the onion and place it with the parsley and 2 glassesful white wine in the hollow dish in which you have put your rabbit or hare.

RECAPITULATION.

VENISON.

ROASTS.

357a.	Selle de Chevreuil................Saddle of Venison.	
357d.	Cuissot de Chevreuil..............Roast leg of Venison.	

RELEVES.

357b. Selle de Chevreuil, Sauce } Saddle of Venison with sauce Poi-
      Poivrade......................... }   vrade.

357c. Selle de Chevreuil, Sauce } Saddle of venison with venison
      Venaison.................. .... }   sauce.

357e. Cuissot de Chevreuil, Sauce } Leg of Venison.   Sauce Poivrade.
      Poivrade......... .... }

357f. Cuissot de Chevreuil, Sauce } Leg of Venison.   Sauce Venison.
      Venaison .... }

ENTREES.

357g. Fillet de Chevreuil, Sauce } Venison steak, sauce venison.
      Venaison .... }

357h. Cotelettes de Chevreuil, } Venison chops or cutlets. Sauce
      Sauce Poivrade................. }   Poivrade.

357i. Civet de Chevreuil.................Venison stew.

HARE.

ROAST.

357j. Rable de Lievre.....................Roast back of Hare.

ENTREE.

357k. Civet de Lievre a la Parisienne. Stew of Hare a la Parisienne.

RABBIT.

ROAST.

357l. Rable de Lapin...... ....Roast back of Rabbit.

ENTREES.

357m. Civet de Lapin.......................Rabbit stew, No. 1.
357n. Gibelotte de Lapin.................Rabbit stew, No. 2.
357o. Lapin Saute Chasseur ....Rabbit Saute a la Chasseur.

WILD TURKEY

ROAST.

357p. Dinde Sauvage Roti.............. Wild Turkey roasted.

ENTREE.

357q. Salmis de Dinde....................Salmis of Turkey.

PRAIRIE CHICKEN, PHEASANT, PARTRIDGE.

ROAST.

357r. Poule de Prairie, Faisant ou } Prairie Chicken, Pheasant or
      Perdrix Roti.................... }   Partridge roasted.

ENTREES.

357s. Poule de Prairie, Faisant ou Perdrix grille.................... } Prairie Chicken, Pheasant or Partridge broiled.

357t. Salmis de Poule de Prairie, Faisant ou de Perdrix......... } Salmis of Prairie Chicken, Pheasant, or Partridge.

WILD DUCK.

ROAST.

357u. Canard Sauvage Roti.............. Wild duck roasted.

ENTREE.

357v. Salmis de Canard Sauvage...... Salmis of Wild Duck.

SMALL BIRDS.

357w. Quail, Snipe, Reed Birds, etc.

SAUCES TO BE SERVED WITH GAME.

357x. Sauce Poivrade.
357y. Sauce Venaison......... .... Venison Sauce.
357z. Pickling No. 1.   Pickling No. 2.

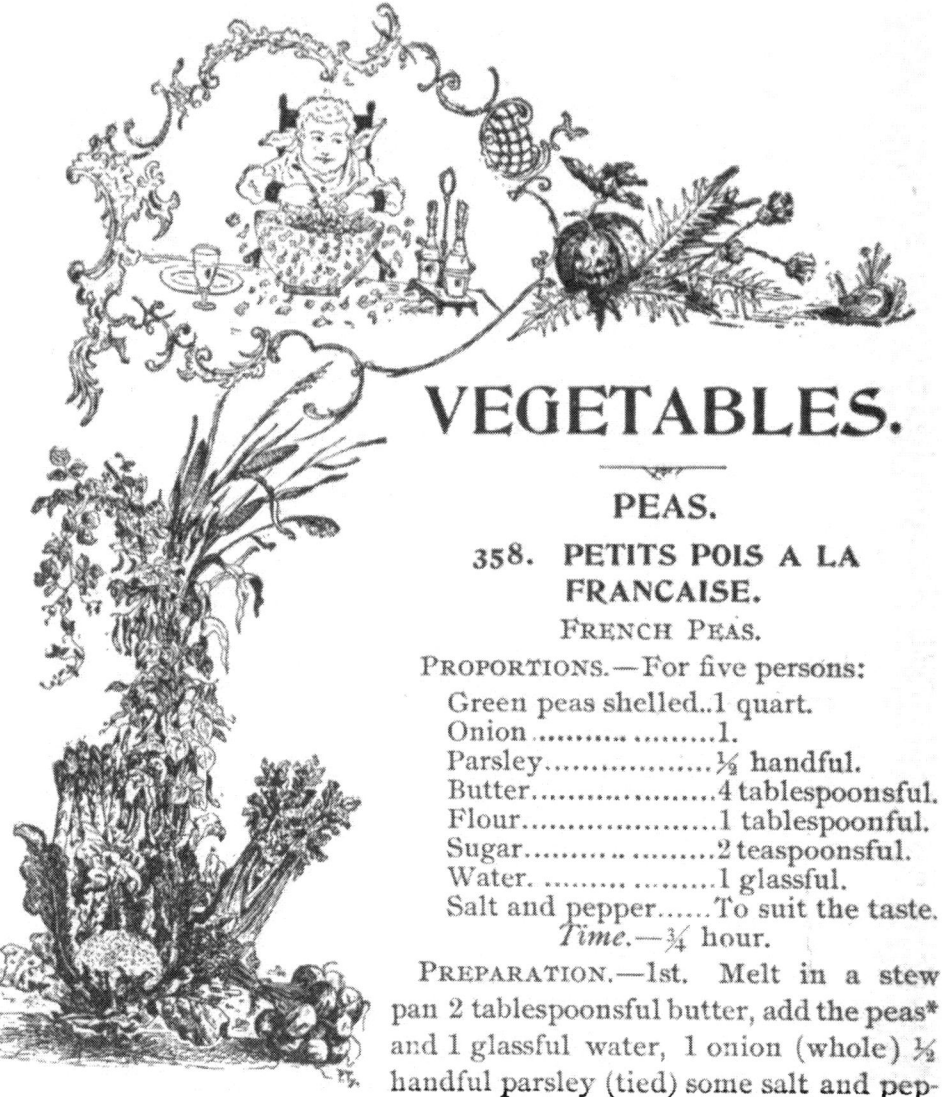

VEGETABLES.

PEAS.

358. PETITS POIS A LA FRANCAISE.

FRENCH PEAS.

PROPORTIONS.—For five persons:

Green peas shelled..1 quart.
Onion ....1.
Parsley.................⅛ handful.
Butter...................4 tablespoonsful.
Flour....................1 tablespoonful.
Sugar........... ....2 teaspoonsful.
Water. ....1 glassful.
Salt and pepper......To suit the taste.
Time.—¾ hour.

PREPARATION.—1st. Melt in a stew pan 2 tablespoonsful butter, add the peas* and 1 glassful water, 1 onion (whole) ⅛ handful parsley (tied) some salt and pepper and cook slowly for about ¾ hour. 2d. When ready to serve take out the onion and the parsley, add 2 tablespoonsful fresh butter mixed with 1 tablespoonful flour and serve in a *warm*, hollow dish as a side dish or as a garnish.

359. PETITS POIS AU LARD.

GREEN PEAS WITH BACON.

PROPORTIONS.—For five persons:

Green peas shelled.1 quart.
Onion ... .1.
Parsley....... ....⅛ handful.
Bacon...................1 lb.
Flour.................1 tablespoonful.
Water ....1 glassful.
Salt and pepper..To suit the taste.
Time.—1 hour.

* Don't select the peas too large because they are old and tough.

PREPARATION.—1st. Cut the bacon in dices and brown awhile in a sauce pan. Sprinkle over 1 tablespoonful flour. 2d. Add 1 glassful water, the peas, 1 onion (whole), ⅓ handful parsley tied, and cook for 1 hour. 3d. When ready to serve take out the onion and the parsley and serve in a warm hollow dish as a side dish.

360. PETITS POIS A L'ANGLAISE.

GREEN PEAS A L'ANGLAISE.

PROPORTIONS.—For five persons:

Green peas.................1 quart. Butter.............................¼ lb.

Time.—20 minutes.

PREPARATION.—1st. Pour the peas in boiling water.* Let them cook quickly for about ¼ of an hour and drip. 2d. Place the peas (dripped) in a warm, hollow dish and place over them ¼ lb. butter divided in small slices (the butter should be melted by the *heat of the peas.*) 3d. Serve as a side dish.

BEANS.

361. HARICOTS VERTS A L'ANGLAISE.

STRING BEANS A L'ANGLAISE.

PROPORTIONS.—For five persons:

String beans.................1 quart. Butter... ....¼ lb.

Time.—20 minutes.

PREPARATION.—1st. Clean the green beans, break off the end that grew at the vine drawing off at the same time the string upon the edge. Repeat the same process from the other end. Break them in two if too long. 2d. Do as indicated, No. 360, and do not forget to cook the beans *quickly* in a *large quantity* of water.

362. HARICOTS VERTS BONNE FEMME.

STRING BEANS A LA BONNE FEMME.

PROPORTIONS.—For five persons:

Green beans...1 quart.	Eggs....................2.
Parsley..........⅓ handful.	Water.....................⅓ glassful.
Onion.............1.	Milk.....................⅓ glassful.
Butter............4 tablespoonsful.	Salt and pepper...To suit the taste.

Time.—1 hour.

---

* Use quite a large quantity of water so that the introduction of the peas does not stop the ebullition. By so doing the peas will remain green.

PREPARATION.—1st. Clean the string beans as indicated, No. 361, 1st. 2d. Melt in a sauce pan two tablespoonsful butter; add the beans, ⅓ glassful water, 1 onion whole, ⅓ handful parsley, some salt and pepper; cook slowly for about ¼ hour. 3d. When ready to serve add 2 table-spoonsful butter and 2 eggs beaten with ⅓ glassful milk. Don't allow to boil, and serve in a *warm* hollow dish as a side dish.

363. GROS SOISSONS AU BEURRE.

LIMA BEANS WITH BUTTER.

PROPORTIONS AND PREPARATION.—As for No. 362.

364. HARICOTS SECS A LA MENAGERE.

KIDNEY BEANS A LA MENAGERE.

PROPORTIONS AND PREPARATION.—As indicated for the "Bretonne," No. 330, but don't use onion.

NOTE.—With the water in which the beans have been cooked you can make a very good family soup by doing as indicated in note of No. 32.

SPINAGE.

365. EPINARDS A LA CREME.

SPINAGE WITH CREAM.

PROPORTIONS.—For five persons:

Spinage ....⅓ peck.	Sugar..............2 teaspoonsful.
Butter...........4 tablespoonsful.	Cream or milk...1 glassful.
Flour. ....1 tablespoonful.	Salt ....A little.

Time.— 30 minutes.

PREPARATION.—1st. Clean and wash 3 or 4 times, about ⅓ peck of spinage; let it cook for 10 minutes in quite a large quantity of salted boiling water. 2d. Take the boiling water off and replace it by cold water till the spinage be cold enough. 3d. Let it drip, and then chop it very fine. 4th. Ten minutes before serving put the spinage in a sauce pan with 4 tablespoonsful butter, 1 tablespoonful flour, a little sugar and salt; let cook awhile, and add while stirring 1 glass milk; serve as side dish or as a garnish.

366. EPINARDS AUX CROUTONS.

SPINAGE WITH TOAST.

PROPORTIONS AND PREPARATION.—As for No. 365, but place on the spinage some toast fried in butter.

367. EPINARDS AUX OEUFS POCHES.

SPINAGE WITH POACHED EGGS.

OPORTIONS AND PREPARATION.—As for No. 365, but place on the spinage 6 eggs poached as indicated, No. 9 *Note.*

CELERY.

368. CELERIS AU JUS.

CELERY WITH GRAVY.

PROPORTIONS.—For five persons:

Celery.........8 small stalks.	Corn starch........1 tablespoonful.
Butter.........2 tablespoonsful.	Salt...................A little.
Stock ....Enough to cover.	*Time.*—1¼ hours.

PREPARATIONS.—1st. Take the lower part of the celery stock (the upper part will be used in celery with cream No. 369.) 2d. Clean the celery, cut it in pieces about 5 inches long, wipe them carefully, place them in a sauce pan, cover with stock add a little salt and cook slowly for 1 hour. 3d. Drip the celery, place it in a hollow dish which you keep in a warm place and boil down the stock in which it has been cooked on a bright fire. 4th. When ready to serve add 1 tablespoonful corn starch mixed with some cold stock and 2 tablespoonsful butter and pour the whole on the celery.

369. CELERIS A LA CREME.

CELERY WITH CREAM.

PROPORTIONS.—For five persons:

Celery............8 stalks.	Milk...............1 glassful.
Butter...........2 tablespoonsful.	Corn starch.....2 tablespoonsful.
	Time.—20 minutes.

PREPARATION.—1st. Take the upper half of the celery instead of the lower part as in No. 368. Wash and cut in pieces 1½ inches long. 2d. Cook in boiling water until tender (about ¼ hour) and drip. 3d. Pour the celery in a sauce pan with 2 tablespoonsful butter, add 1 glassful cold milk or cream in which you have mixed 2 tablespoonsful corn starch. Boil a little while and serve in a hollow dish as a side dish.

CARROTS.

370. CAROTTES NOUVELLES SAUTTEES AU BEURRE.

SMALL CARROTS FRIED IN BUTTER.

PROPORTIONS.—For five persons:

Carrots............3 bunches.
Butter..............2 tablespoonsful.
Sugar................2 teaspoonsful.
Time.—30 minutes.

PREPARATION.—1st.   Pare the carrots (small and young) slice them crosswise as thick as a half dollar and cook in boiling water till tender, about 15 minutes.   2d. Melt in a sauce pan 2 tablespoonsful butter, add the carrots carefully dripped, sprinkle over a little sugar and fry for about 10 minutes. 3d. Serve as a side dish.

371. CAROTTES NOUVELLES A LA CREME.

SMALL CARROTS WITH CREAM.

PROPORTIONS.—For five persons:

Carrots............1 to 1½ quarts.   Sugar...............2 teaspoonsful.
Cream or milk..2 glassesful.   Salt..................A little.
Flour..............1 tablespoonful.   *Time.*—30 minutes.

PREPARATION.—1st. As indicated 1st. No. 370.   2d. Melt in a sauce pan 2 tablespoonsful butter, add the carrots dripped, sprinkle with salt and the sugar, add 1 tablespoonful flour and 2 glassesful cream or milk and cook a little while.   Serve in a warm dish as side dish.

ASPARAGUS.

372. ASPERGES, SAUCE BLANCHE.

ASPARAGUS WITH WHITE SAUCE.

PROPORTIONS.—For five persons.

Asparagus (white).....3 bunches.   Hollandaise sauce........No. 151.
Salt.......................A little.   *Time.*—15 minutes.

PREPARATION.—1st. Clean and wash 3 bunches asparagus.   Cook in boiling, salted water till tender (10 to 15 minutes) and serve on a folded napkin with a Sauce Hollandaise, No. 151, apart.

373. ASPERGES, SAUCE POLONNAISE.

ASPARAGUS WITH POLONNAISE SAUCE.

PROPORTIONS.—For five persons:

sparagus (white).....3 bunches. Butter............¼ lb.
Salt....................A little. Bread crumbs..3 tablespoonsful.
Time.—20 minutes

PREPARATION.—1st. As for No. 372, and serve with a Sauce Polonnaise made as follows: Melt in a sauce pan ¼ lb. butter, add a little salt and 3 tablespoonsful bread crumbs broken fine, brown awhile, but do not let the butter become too dark and pour the sauce in a warm sauce boat.

374. ASPERGES, SAUCE VINAIGRETTE.

ASPARAGUS WITH VINEGAR SAUCE.

PROPORTIONS.—For five persons:

Asparagus (green).....4 bunches. Vinaigrette sauce.........No. 165.
Salt....................A little. *Time.*—20 minutes.

PREPARATION.—1st. Cook the asparagus as indicated No. 372, and serve on a folded napkin with a sauce Vinaigrette, No. 165, apart.

CAULIFLOWER.

375. CHOUX FLEURS, SAUCE BLANCHE.

CAULIFLOWERS WITH WHITE SAUCE.

PROPORTIONS.—For five persons:

Cauliflowers..............2. Hollandaise sauce........No. 151.
Salt......................A little. *Time.*—½ hour.

PREPARATION.—1st. Clean two cauliflowers, cut them in four and wash them carefully. 2d. Let them cook in boiling salted water till tender (about ½ hour). 3d. Drip them and place in a hollow dish in the original shape. Serve with a Hollandaise sauce, No. 151, apart.

376. CHOUX FLEURS, SAUCE POLONAISE.

CAULIFLOWERS WITH SAUCE POLONNAISE.

PROPORTIONS AND PREPARATION.—As for No. 375, and serve with a sauce Polonnaise, No. 373.

377. CHOUX FLEURS AU GRATIN.

CAULIFLOWERS AU GRATIN.

PROPORTIONS.—For five persons:

Cauliflowers....2. Butter............5 tablespoonsful.
Bread crumbs..2 tablespoonsful. Flour.............3 tablespoonsful.
Rasped cheese.2 tablespoonsful. Milk...............1 pint.
Time.—¾ hour.

PREPARATION.--1st As 1st. and 2d., No. 375. 3d. Make a sauce as follows: Melt in a saucepan 2 tablespoonsful butter mixed with 3 tablespoonsful flour, add, while stirring, about 1 pint milk, boil while stirring till the sauce becomes quite thick, and add two tablespoonsful butter. 4th. Pour some of this sauce in the bottom of a hollow dish, add the cauliflower (cut in four or five), pour over the remainder of the cream sauce, sprinkle over some bread crumbs and rasped cheese, brush with some melted butter and bake in an oven till well colored (from 10 to 15 minutes.)

378. CHOUCROUTE A LA STRASBOURGEOISE.

SAUR KROUT A LA STRASBOURGEOISE.

Saur krout	5 lbs.	Carrots	2.
Bacon	1 lb.	Onions	2.
Sausage	1 lb.	Stock	3 glassesful.

Time.—5 hours.

PREPARATION.—1st. Take 5 lbs. saur krout (must be of a clear color). Press in a napkin to remove the greatest part of the pickling. 2d. Place it in a kettle with 1 lb. bacon and 1 lb. sausage, 2 carrots cut in four and 2 whole onions, add 3 glassesful stock and cook slowly for 5 hours. 3d. Drip the saur krout, take out the carrots and the onions, serve in a hollow dish with the bacon cut in slices and placed on top and the sausage around.

TOMATOES.

379. TOMATTES SAUTTES A LA PROVENCALE.

TOMATO SAUTTEES A LA PROVENCALE.

PROPORTIONS.—For five persons:

Tomatoes	12.	Parsley	¼ handful.
Oil	3 tablespoonsful.	Salt and pepper	To suit the taste.
Garlic	1 clove.	Cayenne pepper	A little.

Time.—10 minutes.

PREPARATION.—1st. Warm in a frying pan 3 tablespoonsful olive oil, add the tomatoes sliced, cook on bright fire, add some salt and pepper, 1 garlic clove chopped fine, ¼ handful chopped parsley and a little cayenne pepper, cook for 10 minutes and serve in a hollow dish as a side dish.

380. TOMATTES FARCIES.

STUFFED TOMATOES.

PROPORTIONS.—For five persons:

Tomatoes	12.	Meat	¼ lb.
Onion	1.	Bread	3 oz.
Parsley	¼ handful.	Bread crumbs	2 tablespoonsful.
Butter	4 tablespoonsful.	Milk or stock	1 glassful.

Time.—½ hour.

PREPARATION.—1st. Cut out a small core at the top of the tomato and squeeze slightly with the hand so as to remove some of the seeds and then stuff with a stuffing made as follows: 2d. Chop 1 onion, put it in a saucepan with 2 tablespoonsful flour, 4 oz. chopped meat (already cooked or sausage meat) 3 oz. white bread having been dipped in some milk or stock, a little chopped parsley. Let cook awhile. 3d. Put this stuffing in the tomatoes, pour over some bread crumbs, some rasped cheese, brush over with some melted butter and let bake in an oven for ¼ hour.

CUCUMBERS.

381. CONCUMBRES A LA CREME.

CUCUMBERS WITH CREAM.

PROPORTIONS.—For five persons:

Cucumbers............6.		Sugar...................2 teaspoonsful.	
Butter...................¼ lb.		Salt...... ....A little.	
Cream...................2 glassesful.		*Time.*—20 minutes.	

PREPARATION.—1st. Peel the cucumbers, cut them in four endwise, take the seeds out and cut them in pieces about 2 inches long. 2d. Melt ¼ lb. butter in a shallow stew pan and when warm add the cucumbers. Cook on *bright* fire for about 10 minutes. 3d. Add 2 glassesful cream, a little salt and sugar, boil awhile and serve as a side dish.

MUSHROOMS.*

382. CHAMPIGNONS A LA CREME.

MUSHROOMS WITH CREAM.

PROPORTIONS.—For five persons:

Mushrooms.....2 lb. can.		Cream or milk........1 glassful.	
Yolks.......... ..2.		Parsley.................¼ handful.	
Starch...........1 tablespoonful.		*Time*—15 minutes.	

PREPARATION.—1st. Pour a 2-lb. can of mushrooms in a sauce pan with their juice and boil a while. 2d. Place the sauce pan on a corner of the range and add two yelks mixed in a bowl with 1 tablespoonful corn starch, 1 tablespoonful cream and some chopped parsley. Serve as a garnish for fine dinners

---

* It requires some experience to select fresh mushrooms, therefore we give only recipes for canned ones.

383. ÇROUTE AUX CHAMPIGNONS.

MUSHROOMS ON TOAST.

PROPORTIONS.—As for No. 382 and

Butter.................3 tablespoonful.	Toasts...........................8 to 10	
Rasped cheese.....3 tablespoonful.	*Time.*—⅓ hour.	

PREPARATION.—1st. Prepare 8 or 10 toasts 5 inches long, 3 inches wide and 1¼ inches thick. 2d. Make a hole in each 4 inches long, 2 inches wide and 1 inch deep, and fry them in butter. 3d. Place the toast on a buttered dish and add in each some mushrooms prepared as indicted, No. 382. 4th. Sprinkle over some rasped cheese, brush with some melted butter and bake in an oven for 10 minutes.

MAIS OR SWEET CORN.

384. MAIS A L'AMERICAINE.

SWEET CORN WITH BUTTER.

PROPORTIONS.—For five persons.

Ears of young corn....10.	Butter............................¼ lb.
Milk.......................1 glassful.	*Time.*—30 minutes.

PREPARATION.—1st. Clean and wash the corn and let it cook in salted boiling water to which you have added 1 glassful milk for ½ hour. 2d. Serve on a folded napkin with some fresh butter apart.

385. MAIS GRILLE.

BROILED SWEETCORN.

PROPORTIONS.—Same as above, No. 384.

PREPARATION.—1st. As 1st., No. 384. 2d. Broil on a bright fire and serve with fresh butter apart.

386. MAIS A LA CREME.

SWEET CORN WITH CREAM.

PROPORTIONS.—For five persons.

Sweet corn......1 lb. can.	Corn starch....1 tablespoonful.
Butter............1 tablespoonful.	Cream...........1 glassful.
Time.—¼ hour.	

PREPARATION.—1st. Drip 1 lb. can of sweet corn. Place it in a sauce pan with 1 tablespoonful butter, warm, add ½ glassful cream or milk. boil awhile, and add the remainder of the cream or milk mixed with 1 tablespoonful corn starch. Warm and serve as a side dish or a garnish.

387. GALETTE DE MAIS

CORN MEAL GALETTE.

PROPORTIONS.—For five persons:

Corn meal	1 lb.		To cook ......10 minutes.
Milk	1 quart.	*Time.*—	To cool........ 2 minutes.
Butter	½ lb.		To fry.........10 minutes.

PREPARATION.—1st. Pour in a sauce pan 1 lb. corn meal which you mix with 1 quart milk and cook for ten minutes while stirring. 2d. Pour this pap in two or more table plates and let cool. 3d. Take 2 frying pans, melt in each about 1 tablespoonful butter, and slip the pap from the plate into the pan. Fry for five minutes. 3d. Slip the "galette" into the plates and again in the pan, turning it over. This is the easiest way to turn a "galette" without breaking it. 4th. Fry the second side for five minutes and serve with some fresh butter apart.

388. POMMES DE TERRE SUCREES EN ROBE DE CHAMBRE.

SWEET POTATOES BOILED.

PROPORTIONS.—For five persons:

Sweet potatoes..................12. Butter.........................¼ lb.
Time.—30 minutes.

PREPARATION.—1st. Wash the potatoes; cut off the ends and let them boil till tender in salted water, about ½ hour. 2d. Serve on a folded napkin with some fresh butter apart.

389. POMMES DE TERRE SUCREES SAUTTEES.

SWEET POTATOES FRIED IN BUTTER.

PROPORTIONS.—For five persons:

Boiled sweet potatoes ....12. Butter............2 tablespoonsful.
Time.—10 minutes.

PREPARATION.—1st. Cook the potatoes as indicated, No. 388; peel them, slice them and fry in butter.

390. POMMES DE TERRE EN ROBE DE CHAMBRE.

POTATOES BOILED.

PROPORTIONS AND PREPARATION.—As for No. 388, but don't cut off the ends.

391. POMMES DE TERRE AU FOUR.

BAKED POTATOES.

PROPORTIONS.—For five persons:

Potatoes ....12. Butter ....¼ lb.
Time.—½ hour.

PREPARATION —Wash the potatoes; place them in a stove pan; let them bake in an oven for ½ hour, and serve with fresh butter apart

392. POMMES DE TERRE SAUTTEES.

POTATOES FRIED IN BUTTER.

PROPORTIONS AND PREPARATION.—As for the sweet potatoes fried in butter, No. 389.

393. POMMES DE TERRE A LA CREME.

POTATOES WITH CREAM.

PROPORTIONS.—For five persons:

Boiled potatoes..12.	Chopped parsley..¼ handful.
Butter...............2 tablespoonsful.	Salt and pepper...To suit the taste.
Cream ....2 glassesful.	*Time.*—10 minutes.

PREPARATION.—Slice the boiled potatoes; place them in a sauce pan with two tablespoonsful butter and 2 glassesful cream; sprinkle over some salt and pepper and some chopped parsley and boil for 10 minutes.

394. POMMES DE TERRE AU GRATIN.

POTATOES AU GRATIN.

PROPORTIONS.—As for No. 393, and

Butter...............2 tablespoonsful.	Rasped cheese..2 tablespoonsful.
	Time.—20 minutes.

PREPARATION.—Prepare the potatoes as in No. 393; place them in a dish; sprinkle over some rasped cheese; brush over with butter; place in an oven and let bake till well colored.

395. PUREE DE POMMES DE TERRE.

MASHED POTATOES.

PROPORTIONS.—For five persons:

Potatoes.................10.	Butter...........2 tablespoonsful.
Cream ....1 glassful.	*Time.*—15 minutes.

PREPARATION.—1st. Peel the potatoes, slice them, place them in a sauce pan with enough water to cover them (no more), and cook till tender (about 10 minutes). 2d. Let them drip; place them in a warm sauce pan and mash (with a fork or potato-masher) with 2 tablespoonsful butter; add 1 glassful cream; let warm, but not boil, and serve as a side dish or a garnish.

396. POMMES DE TERRE DUCHESSE.

POTATOES DUCHESSE.

PROPORTIONS.—For five persons:

Potatoes	10.	Flour	2 tablespoonsful.
Yelks	3.	Butter	Enough to fry.

Time.—30 minutes.

PREPARATION.—1st. As 1st., No. 395. 2d. Let them drip and place them in a warm sauce pan; mash with 3 yelks so as to obtain quite a thick pap. 3d. Place the pap on a table on which you have sprinkled some flour; roll it and divide in small cakes about 3 inches long, 1½ inches wide and ¾ inch thick; fry in butter on both sides and serve as a garnish for tenderloin, veal, saddle of mutton, etc.

397. CROQUETTES DE POMMES DE TERRE.

POTATO CROQUETTES.

PROPORTIONS.—Same as for No. 396, and

Eggs	2.	Butter	1 tablespoonful
Bread crumbs	4 tablespoonsful.	*Time.*—30 minutes.	

PREPARATION.—1st. and 2d. as for No. 396, but add 1 tablespoonful butter while mashing; roll them in the shape of small cylinder 3 inches long and 1¼ inches thick. 2d. Dip them in a beaten egg; roll in bread crumbs and fry in butter; serve for lunch or as a garnish.

398. POMME DE TERRE AU LARD.

POTATOES WITH BACON.

PROPORTIONS.—For five persons:

Potatoes	12 to 15.	Parsley	½ handful.
Bacon	1 lb.	Stock or water	1 glassful.
Flour	1 tablespoonful.	Salt and pepper	To suit the taste.

Time.—½ hour.

PREPARATION.—1st. Cut the bacon in dices, fry a little in a stew pan, then sprinkle over 1 tablespoonful flour, add 2 glassesful stock or water, and the potatoes peeled and cut in 2, 4, or 6 according to the size, some salt and pepper and some parsley, tied, cook slowly for ½ hour and serve on a hollow warm dish.

399. POMMES DE TERRE FARCIES.

STUFFED POTATOES.

PROPORTIONS.—For 5 persons:

Potatoes	6 to 8.	Yelks	2.
Butter	4 tablespoonsful.	Cream	¼ glassful.

Time.—¾ hour.

PREPARATION.—1st. Wash 6 or 8 nice long potatoes, let them bake as indicated No. 397. 2d. Cut the potatoes in two, endwise, take out all the flesh, place it in a sauce pan where you mash it with 2 table-spoonsful butter, 2 yelks, ½ glassful cream and a little salt. Fill the potato skins with this pap, rub them with melted butter and bake for 10 minutes.

400. POMMES DE TERRE FRITTES.

FRIED POTATOES.

PROPORTIONS.—For five persons:

Potatoes...........................12.   Fat..................Enough to fry.
Salt..................To suit the taste.

PREPARATION.—To fry potatoes it is necessary to have quite a large quantity of fat or lard; while the fat heats, peel the potatoes, slice them and fry till well colored.

401. POMMES DE TERRE SOUFFLEES.

PUFFED POTATOES.

PROPORTIONS.—Same as No. 400

PREPARATION.—1st. Peel the potatoes, cut them endwise in slices about ¼ inch thick. 2d. Put them in warm but not hot fat. Let them cook till tender (10 minutes.)* 3d. Take the potatoes from the fat, let them drip and put them aside. 4th. Heat the fat very hot and pour the potatoes in it again, and fry quickly. They will puff and have a very nice appearance.

MACARONI.

402. MACARONI A L'ITALIENNE.

PROPORTIONS.—For five persons:

Macaroni......1 lb.   Cheese...........................½ lb.
Butter..........4 tablespoonsful.   *Time.*—20 minutes.

PREPARATION.—1st. Cook the macaroni in some salted water (don't fear to put in too much water), till quite soft, let it drip, throw the water away and replace the macaroni in the same kettle in which it had been cooked (this is empty now but *warm*), add 4 tablespoonsful butter, ½ lb. rasped cheese, some salt and pepper; allow the butter and the cheese to melt while stirring, but don't place the kettle on the range again. By doing so, the butter and the cheese remain half melted, and the macaroni is very palatable.

---

* The fat should not be warm enough to fry.

403. MACARONI SAUCE TOMATE.

MACARONI WITH TOMATO SAUCE.

PROPORTIONS AND PREPARATION.—As for No. 402, and add three table-spoonsful tomato catsup.

404. MACARONI AU GRATIN.

MACARONI AU GRATIN.

PROPORTIONS.—As for No. 402 and

Bread crumbs...2 tablespoonsful.   Butter..........1 tablespoonful.
Rasped cheese............3 tablespoonsful.

PREPARATION.—1st. Do as indicated for No. 402. 2d. Place the macaroni on a dish, pour over it some bread crumbs and rasped cheese, brush over with melted butter and let it bake in an oven till well colored.

405. RIZ A LA MILANAISE.

RICE A LA MILANAISE.

PROPORTIONS.—For five persons:

Rice................................1 lb.   Butter........................¼ lb.
Onion..............................1.   Cheese........................¼ lb.
Time.—½ hour.

PREPARATION.—1st. Wash 1 lb. of rice in cold water several times till the water is clear. 2d. Cook it in boiling water till quite soft.* 3d. Let it drip, cool and drip again. 4th. Place in a sauce pan 1 chopped onion with ¼ lb. butter, let it brown awhile, add the rice and ¼ lb. rasped cheese and mix well (with 2 forks so as not to break the rice). 5th. Cover the pan and let it bake in an oven for ¼ hour. Serve in a hollow dish as a side dish.

406. RIZ A LA GEORGIENNE.

RICE A LA GEORGIENNE.

PROPORTIONS.—For five persons:

Rice...........................1 lb.   Butter........................¼ lb.
Time.—¼ hour.

PREPARATION.—1st., 2d. and 3d. as for No. 405. 4th. Melt in a sauce pan ¼ lb. butter, add the rice and some salt and pepper. 5th. Mix well, cover the sauce pan and bake in an oven for ¼ hour. Serve as a side dish or as a garnish.

---

* The rice will be done when you can cut it easily with your finger nail, but before the grains are so soft as to mash between the fingers.

407. RIZ A LA CREOLE

Rice a la Creole.

PROPORTIONS.—For five persons:

Rice	1 lb.	Garlic	1 clove.
Butter	¼ lb.	Ham	½ lb.
Tomatoes	6.	Parsley	¼ lb.
Onion	1.		

*Time.—*½ hour.

PREPARATION.—1st., 2d. and 3d. as indicated No. 405. 4th. Melt in a sauce pan ¼ lb. butter, add 1 chopped onion, ½ lb. ham cut in dices, and brown awhile. 5th. Add some chopped parsley, 1 garlic clove, 6 tomatoes cut in dices, brown again. 6th. Add a little cayenne pepper, cook the whole for five minutes and mix as in No. 405.

408. OAT MEAL A L'AMERICAINE.

Oat Meal a l'Americaine.

PROPORTIONS.—For five persons:

Oat meal	1 lb.	Salt	To suit the taste.
Butter	1 tablespoonful.		

*Time.—*¼ hour.

PREPARATION.—1st. Mix in a sauce pan 1 lb. oat meal with 1 tablespoonful butter, 1 pint water and some salt. 2d. Bake in an oven for ¼ hour and serve with some butter and milk or cream apart.

409. CROQUETTES DE OAT MEAL.

Oat Meal Croquettes.

PROPORTIONS AND PREPARATION.—As indicated, No. 408, and make croquettes as indicated, No. 397.

410. GALETTE DE OAT MEAL.

Oat Meal Galette.

PROPORTIONS AND PREPARATION.—1st. Do as indicated at No. 408 then as indicated for the galette of corn, No. 387.

RECAPITULATION.

PEAS.

358. Petits Pois a la Francaise ....French Peas.
359. Petits Pois au Lard..................Green Peas with Bacon.
360. Petits Pois a l'Anglaise...........Green Peas a l'Anglaise.

BEANS.

361. Haricots Verts a l'Anglaise......String Beans a l'Anglaise.
362. Haricots Verts Bonne Femme...String Beans a la Bonne Femme.
363. Gros Soissons au Beurre..........Lima Beans with Butter.
364. Haricots Secs Menagere...........Kidney Beans a la Menagere.

SPINAGE.

365. Epinards a la Creme ... .Spinage with Cream.
366. Epinards aux Croutons...........Spinage with Toast.
367. Epinards aux Oeufs Poches......Spinage with Poached Eggs.

CELERY.

368. Celeris aux Jus.......................Celery with Gravy.
369. Celeris a la Creme ....Celery with Cream.

CARROTS.

370. Carottes Nouvelles Sautees au } Small Carrots Fried in Butter.
    Beurre............................. }
371. Carottes Nouvelles a la Creme...Small Carrots with Cream.
328. Carottes a la Nivernaise...........Carrots a la Nivernaise.

ASPARAGUS.

372. Asperges Sauce Blanche..........Asparagus with White Sauce.
373. Asperges Sauce Polonnaise ......Asparagus with Polonnaise Sauce.
374. Asperges Sauce Vinaigrette......Asparagus with Vinegar Sauce.

CAULIFLOWERS.

375. Choux Fleurs Sauce Blanche....Cauliflowers with White Sauce.
376. Choux Fleurs Sauce Polonnaise.Cauliflowers with Polonnaise Sauce.
377. Choux Fleurs au Gratin ....Cauliflowers au Gratin.
329. Choux a la Flamande..............Cabbage a la Flamande.
378. Choucroute a la Strasbourgeoise Saur Krout a la Strasbourgeoise.

TOMATOES.

379. Tomattes Sauttecs a la Pro- } Tomatoes Sauttees a la Provencale.
    vencale........................... }
380. Tomattes Farcies....................Stuffed Tomatoes.

CUCUMBERS.

381. Concombres a la Creme...........Cucumbers with Cream.

MUSHROOMS.

382. Champignons a la Creme.........Mushrooms with Cream.
383. Croute aux Champignons.........Mushrooms on Toast.

SWEET CORN.

384. Mais a l'Americaine................Sweet Corn with Butter.
385. Mais Grille.............................Broiled Sweet Corn.
386. Mais a la Creme ....Sweet Corn with Cream.
387. Galette de Mais......................Galette of Corn.

POTATOES.

388. Pommes de Terre Sucrees en Robe de Chambre............. } Boiled Sweet Potatoes.
389. Pommes de Terre Sucrees Sauttees.......................... } Sweet Potatoes Fried in Butter.
390. Pommes de Terre en Robe de Chambre...................... } Boiled Potatoes.
391. Pommes de Terre au Four.......Baked Potatoes.
392. Pommes de Terre Sauttees.......Potatoes Fried in Butter.
393. Pommes de Terre a la Creme.....Potatoes with Cream.
394. Pommes de Terre au Gratin.......Potatoes au Gratin.
395. Puree de Pommes de Terre........Mashed Potatoes.
396. Pommes de Terre Duchesse......Potatoes Duchesse.
397. Croquettes de Pommes de Terre.Potato Croquettes.
398. Pommes de Terre au Lard... ....Potatoes with Bacon.
399. Pommes de Terre Farcies ....Stuffed Potatoes.
400. Pommes de Terre Frittes.........Fried Potatoes.
401. Pommes de Terre Souffles........Puffed Potatoes.

MACARONI.

402. Macaroni a l'Italienne ....Macaroni a l'Italienne.
403. Macaroni Sauce Tomate...........Macaroni with Tomate Sauce.
404. Macaroni au Gratin ....Macaroni au Gratin.

RICE.

405. Riz a la Milanaise....................Rice a la Milanaise.
406. Riz a la Georgienne.................Rice a la Georgienne.
407 Riz a la Creole........................Rice a la Creole

OATMEAL.

408. Oat Meal a l'Americaine..........Oat Meal a l'Americaine.
409. Croquettes de Oat Meal ....Oat Meal Croquettes.
410. Galette de Oat Meal................Galette of Oat Meal.

SWEET DISHES.

I. WARM SWEET DISHES.

411. PECHES A LA CONDE.

PEACHES A LA CONDE.

PROPORTIONS.—For five persons:

Peaches { canned ......1 lb. can.
{ fresh .... 6.
Rice..............½ lb.
Milk..............2 glassesful.
Sugar............3 or 6 table-
spoonsful.
Lemon............The yellow rind
of one.
Apricot sauce...1 glassful.
Time.—¾ hour.

PREPARATION.—1st. Take 1 lb. can of peaches, peel them, let them drip and put the syrup aside; or, cut the fresh peaches in two, let them cook till tender in some water with 3 tablespoonsful sugar and the yellow rind of a lemon. 2d. Wash ½ lb. rice, let it cook, drip, cool and drip again, as indicated No. 405. 3d. Warm it with 2 glassesful milk, 3 tablespoonsful sugar and the yellow rind of a lemon. 4th. Put the rice in a hollow dish, arrange the peaches in a crown shape and pour over a sauce composed of some apricot jelly and the juice of the peaches.

412. POIRES A LA CONDE.

PEARS A LA CONDE, and

413. ANANAS A LA CREOLE.

PINE APPLE A LA CREOLE.

PROPORTIONS AND PREPARATION.—As for 411, but use pears or pine-apples instead of peaches.

414. PECHES A LA BOURDALOUE.

PEACHES A LA BOURDALOUE.

PROPORTIONS.—For five persons:

Peaches { canned...⅛ lb. can.	Eggs..........3.	
{ fresh......6.	Flour.........3 tablespoonsful.	
Kirsch ....2 tablespoonsful.	Sugar.........3 tablespoonsful.	
Apricot sauce..1 glassful.	Lemon ......Yellow rind of one.	
Milk..............1 pint.	*Time.*—½ hour.	

PREPARATION.—1st. As 1st., No. 411, but do not let the peaches drip and add 2 tablespoonsful kirsch and 1 glassful apricot marmalade to the juice. Place the sauce pan aside on a corner of the range or in a warm, but not hot place. 2d. Make a Bourdaloue as follows: Break 3 eggs in a sauce pan, add 3 tablespoonsful flour, 3 tablespoonsful sugar, the yellow rind of a lemon, beat the whole and add little by little and while beating 1 pint milk, and cook till quite thick (about 10 minutes). Pour this pap in a hollow dish, and bake in an oven till a crust is formed over. 4th. Place the peaches in a crown and pour over the syrup.

415. SOUFFLE A LA VANILLE.

PROPORTIONS.—For five persons:

Eggs.......................3.	Flour......3 tablespoonsful.
Milk ....1 pint.	Vanilla...A little.
Sugar......................⅛ lb.	Lemon ...The yellow rind of one.
Time.—½ hour.	

PREPARATION.—1st. Break 3 eggs, put the white apart and the yelks in a sauce pan. 2d. Add in this sauce pan ⅛ lb. sugar, 3 tablespoonsful flour, some vanilla, the yellow peel (zest) of a lemon, 1 pint milk, allow it to cook while beating till thick enough (about 10 minutes). 2d. Beat the whites and pour in the sauce pan little by little. 3d. Pour the whole in a buttered cake-mould, and allow it to bake in an oven (not too warm) till it swells, and has a nice, yellow color. Serve with some granulated sugar sprinkled over it.

416. SOUFFLE AU OAT MEAL.

PROPORTIONS.—For five persons:

Oat meal ....½ lb.   Milk............... .1 pint.
Sugar................¼ lb.   Eggs................3.
Butter ....1 tablespoonful. Baking powder..1 tablespoonful.
                    Time. -½ hour.

PREPARATION.—1st.   Mix in a sauce pan ½ lb. oatmeal with 1 table spoonful butter, ¼ lb. sugar, 1 pint milk, some vanilla or the yellow rind of a lemon, and cook slowly for 10 minutes.   2d.   Put the sauce pan on the corner of the range, add while stirring 3 eggs and 1 tablespoonful baking powder.   3d.   As 3d., No. 415.

417. SOUFFLE A LA AMERICAINE.

PROPORTIONS.—For five persons:

Eggs.............4.   Milk...... ....1 pint.
Flour ....6 tablespoonsful. Baking powder.1 tablespoonful.
Sugar ....4 tablespoonsful. *Time.*—1½ hours.

PREPARATION.—1st.   Mix together in a bowl 4 eggs, 6 tablespoonsful flour, 4 tablespoonsful sugar, 1 tablespoonful baking powder.   2d.   Add while beating and little by little 1 pint milk. Allow the dough thus made to rest for 1 hour.   3d.   Pour it in a buttered sauce pan or cake mould (this will appear on the table) and bake in an oven till it swells.   Serve with some granulated sugar.

418. POUDDING AU RIZ.

RICE PUDDING.

PROPORTIONS.—For five persons:

Rice..½ lb.
Milk ....1 pint.
          ⎰ Malaga.......................................1 tablespoonful.
Raisins ⎱ Sultana...1 tablespoonful.
          ⎱ Corinth...1 tablespoonful.
Dried orange or lemon peel cut in dices...............1 tablespoonful.
Sugar...¼ lb.
Butter..1 tablespoonful.
                    Time.—1 hour.

PREPARATION.—1st.   Wash, cook, drip, cool and drip again the rice as indicated, No. 405.   Pour the rice in a sauce pan with 1 pint milk, 3 tablespoonsful raisins (Malaga, Sultana and Corinth), 1 tablespoonful dried orange or lemon peel cut in dices, cook slowly for ¼ of an hour. 3d.   Add 3 eggs, stir well and pour in a buttered cake mould. 4th. Bake till well colored, knock it out and serve with a Sambayon or apricot sauce.

419. POUDDING DIPLOMATE.

PROPORTIONS.—For five persons:

Raisins	Malaga.................2 oz.	Eggs............5.	
	Sultana.................2 oz.	Corn starch...1 tablespoonful.	
	Corinth...............2 oz.	Milk...........2 glassesful.	
Lemon or orange peel...........2 oz.		Rum...........1 or 2 tablespoonsful.	
Lady fingers.......................¼ lb.		Sugar..........4 tablespoonsful.	

PREPARATION.—1st. In a cake-mould put a row of dried grapes (if possible, Malaga, Smyrna or Corinth), and dices of preserved orange peel, then a row of lady fingers, then a row of grapes and so on, the last row being a row of lady fingers. Don't fill the mould. 2d. Make a sauce with 5 eggs, 1 tablespoonful corn starch, two glassesful milk, 1 or 2 tablespoonsful rum, 4 tablespoonsful sugar and mix the whole. 3d. Pour this sauce in the mould, put in a bain-marie and bake in an oven (not too warm). 4th. Knock out the pudding on a dish and serve with a Sambayon sauce, No. 430.

420. PLUM PUDDING.

PROPORTIONS.—For five persons:

Kidney fat..¼ lb.		
Raisins	Malaga...2 oz.	
	Smyrna............ ....2 oz.	
	Corinth.......................................2 oz.	
Dices of preserved lemon or orange peel.......2 oz.		
Flour...4 oz.		
Bread...¼ lb.		
Sugar (brown)..¼ lb.		
Apples...3.		
Milk...1 glassful.		
Rum...¼ glassful.		
Salt..A little.		
Cinnamon..A little.		

Time.—5 hours.

PREPARATION.—1st. Place the whole in a large bowl, the fat having been chopped fine and the apples peeled and cut in dices, and beat well with a wooden kitchen spoon. 2d. Butter a napkin and powder with flour inside; place it in a bowl, the buttered part inside, and so as to form a hole, in which you pour the pudding. 3d. Bind the napkin with twine, and let pudding boil for 5 hours in a kettle full of water. 4th. When ready to serve, let it drip in a strainer, take the napkin off, place the pudding on a dish hollow enough to con-

tain ½ pint of rum; sprinkle over it some granulated sugar, pour the rum and light it up. Persons who do not like liquors may serve the pudding with a Sambayon sauce. No. 330.

421. CHARLOTTE DE POMMES.

CHARLOTTE OF APPLES.

PROPORTIONS.—For five persons:

Apples	12.	Cinnamon	A little.
Butter	⅛ lb.	Bread	⅛ lb.
Sugar	¼ lb.	*Time.*—¼ hour.	

PREPARATION.—1st. Peel 12 nice apples, cut them in four, core and slice them fine. 2d. Melt in a sauce pan ¼ lb. butter, add the apples and ¼ lb. sugar, and a little pulverized cinnamon, cook on a bright fire till the apples are soft. 3d. Slice enough bread to line the cake mould and fry the slices in butter. 4th. Line a cake mould with the slices of bread, pour in the apples, bake for ¼ hour in an oven, knock out and serve with an apricot sauce.

422. CROUTE AU MADERE.

TOAST WITH MADEIRA SAUCE.

PROPORTIONS.—For five persons:

Bread	¼ lb.	Rum	½ glassful.
Butter	3 tablespoonsful.	Or	
Apricot sauce	2 glassesful.	Madeira	1 glassful.

PREPARATION.—1st. Slice the bread, fry it in butter, arrange the slices in a crown on a dish and when ready to serve pour over a sauce made as follows: 2d. Mix 2 glassesful apricot sauce with 1 glassful madeira or ½ glassful rum.

423. PAIN PERDU.

PROPORTIONS.—For five persons:

Bread........½ lb.

PROPORTIONS AND PREPARATION.—As for No. 422, but pour over a sauce Sambayon.

424. POMMES FRITTES.

FRIED APPLES.

PROPORTIONS.—For five persons:

Apples	6.	Milk	1 glassful.
Sugar	¼ lb.	Flour	4 tablespoonsful.
Fat	Enough to fry.	*Time.*—20 minutes.	

PREPARATION.—Pare the apples, slice them crosswise ¼ inch thick, dip them in milk, roll in flour and fry till well colored. Sprinkle over some granulated sugar and serve on a folded napkin.

425. PECHES FRITTES.

FRIED PEACHES. AND

426. ANANAS FRIT.

FRIED PINEAPPLE.

PROPORTIONS AND PREPARATION.—As for No. 424, but cut the peaches in 2 or 4, according to the size and don't peel them. Cut the pine apples in slices ¼ inch thick.

427. CREMES FRITTES.

FRIED CREAM.

PROPORTIONS.—For five persons:

Eggs	5.	Milk	1 pint.
Flour	3 tablespoonsful.	Lemon	The yellow rind of 1.
Sugar	2 tablespoonsful.	Vanilla	A little.
		Fat	Enough to fry.

PREPARATION.—1st.—Take 3 eggs, 3 tablespoonsful flour, 2 tablespoonsful sugar, the zest of a lemon, or some vanilla, mix all together. 2d. Add little by little and while beating, 1 pt. boiling milk, till you obtain a thick pap; allow it to cook for 10 minutes, always stirring. 3d. Pour this on a plate in a ⅙ inch layer and let it cool. 4th. Cut the cold pap in cakes, steep them in 2 beaten eggs, roll in bread crumbs and fry. 5th. Serve on a napkin, with granulated sugar.

428. POMMES AU BEURRE.

APPLES WITH BUTTER.

PROPORTIONS.—For five persons:

Apples	8.	Sugar	3 tablespoonsful.
Apricot sauce	1 glassful.		

PREPARATION.—1st. Pare and core 8 nice apples, and dispose them on a buttered dish. 2d. Sprinkle sugar over them and let them bake in an oven until soft. 3d. Prepare a hot syrup with some marmalade of apricot and water, and pour over the apples.

429. POMMES AU FOUR.

BAKED APPLES.

PROPORTIONS AND PREPARATION.—As for No. 428, but do not peel the apples. Core them, put some granulated sugar in the hole and let them bake. When ready to serve, sprinkle some granulated sugar over.

430. SAUCE SAMBAYON.

SAMBAYON SAUCE.

PROPORTIONS.—For five persons:

Yelks	2.	Rum	1 tablespoonful.
Starch	⅓ tablespoonful.	Cream	2 glassesful.
Sugar	2 tablespoonsful.	*Time.*—10 minutes.	

PREPARATION.—1st. In a sauce pan beat together 2 yelks, ⅓ tablespoonful corn starch, 2 tablespoonsful sugar, 1 tablespoonful rum, 2 glassesful cream till thick enough, and warm but don't allow it to boil. 2d. Pour on the pudding.

431. SAUCE APRICOT.

APRICOT SAUCE.

PROPORTIONS.—For five persons:

Apricots	12.	Kirsch	2 tablespoonsful.
Sugar	½ lb.	*Time.*—15 minutes.	

PREPARATION.—1st. Place in a sauce pan 12 apricots cut in pieces with ½ lb. sugar, and cook till soft. 2d. Pass through a sifter, add 2 tablespoonsful kirsch and enough water to have a half thick sauce; or, mix 2 tablespoonsful apricot marmalade with 2 tablespoonsful kirsch and add enough water to make quite a thick sauce.

COLD SWEET DISHES.

432. RIZ A L'IMPERATRICE.

RICE A L'IMPERATRICE.

PROPORTIONS.—For five persons:

Rice	½ lb.	Sugar	¼ lb.
Gelatine	¼ lb.	Cream	2 glassesful.
Vanilla or yellow lemon peel	A little.		

PREPARATION.—1st. Wash, cook, drip, cool and drip again the rice as indicated No. 405. 2d. Place it in a sauce pan with ¼ lb. gelatine, which you have soaked for 10 minutes in cold water and then melted in a sauce pan,* add 2 glassesful cream and cook while stirring for 10 minutes. 3d. Pour this in a cake mould, which you place in an ice box till cold. 4th. When ready to serve knock it from the mould and pour over a raspberry sauce made as follows: 5th. Pass 2 lbs. raspberries through a sifter and mix with ¾ lb. sugar.

*Add a little water if the gelatine is too thick.

433. BLANC MANGER.

PROPORTIONS.—For five persons:

Almonds................1 lb. Gelatine....................¼ lb.
Sugar..........................⅛ lb.

PREPARATION.—1st. Skin the almonds by dipping them in boiling water till the skin is tender, drip, cool in cold water and drip again, then take off the skins. 2d. Break the almonds in a mortar with ¼ lb. sugar, adding, while breaking, a little water. 3d. Place them in a bowl, add ¼ lb. sugar, 1 pint milk, and press through a napkin by turning in an opposite direction (this must be done by two persons). 4th. Add to this almond juice ¼ lb. gelatine melted as indicated, No. 432, pour the whole in a cake mould and cool as indicated, No. 432.

434. KISSEL A LA RUSSE.

PROPORTIONS.—For five persons:

Cranberries...............2 quarts. Starch..........4 tablespoonsful.
Sugar.......................⅛ lb. Cream...........1 pint.

PREPARATION.—1st. Press the cranberries or raspberries through a napkin, pour their juice in a sauce pan with ⅛ lb. sugar, add 4 tablespoonsful corn starch mixed with 1 glassful water, boil the whole for 5 minutes. 2d. Pour in a hollow dish and let cool. Serve with cream apart.

435. CREME AU CHOCOLAT.

PROPORTIONS.—For five persons:

Chocolate...................⅛ lb. Sugar............6 tablespoonsful.
Milk..........................1 quart. Starch...........2 tablespoonsful.
Yelks........................6.

PREPARATION.—1st. Break ⅛ lb. chocolate and put it, while beating with a whip, in 1 quart boiling milk. 2d. Mix apart 6 yelks with 6 tablespoonsful granulated sugar in a sauce pan and pour the chocolate and 2 tablespoonsful corn starch in while stirring. 3d. Pour this cream in a buttered mould and let cook in a *bain marie* for ½ hour. 4th. Knock out on a dish and serve iced.

5th. Serve with a chocolate sauce made as follows:

Chocolate.................¼ lb. Starch............1 tablespoonful.
Water.....................1 glassful. Cream or milk.1 glassful.
Yelks....................4.

PREPARATION.—1st. Melt the chocolate in 1 glassful water. 2d. Place the yelks in a sauce pan with ½ glassful cream, and warm a little; add 1 tablespoonful starch mixed with ½ glassful cream, and add the chocolate while stirring; warm again, but don't let boil; cool and serve with the Creme au Chocolat.

436. CREME AU CAFE.

As for No. 435, but use 4 tablespoonsful coffee for the cream and 2 tablespoonsful for the sauce.

437. CHARLOTTE RUSSE.

PROPORTIONS.—For five persons:

Cream..................1 quart.   Lady fingers....................1 lb.
Sugar........................¼ lb.

PREPARATION.—1st. Line the bottom and the sides of a cake mould with lady fingers. 2d. Whip 1 quart cream (thick cream), and when the cream is whipped sprinkle the sugar over; mix carefully; pour in mould; let cool a little while and knock out.

438. MACEDOINE DE FRUIT.

PROPORTIONS.—For five persons:

Canned	Peaches......... Apricots... ..... Plums............. Cherries......... Pineapples.....	¼ lb. of each.
Sugar..........................		2 tablespoonsful.
Kirsch		1 glassful.

1st. Take ¼ lb. each of preserved peaches, apricots, plums, cherries, pineapples; let drip separately; arrange the fruits in hollow dish so as to have a pretty effect. 2d. Add some sugar to the juice of the fruits; let it simmer down, and when the syrup is concentrated enough let it cool. 3d. When ready to serve add 2 tablespoonsful of maraschino or kirschwasser, and pour the syrup on the fruits.

RECAPITULATION.

Warm Sweet Dishes.

411. Peches a la Conde............. ....Peaches a la Conde.
412. Poires a la Conde.............. ....Pears a la Conde.
413. Ananas a la Creole..................Pine Apple a la Creole.
414. Peches a la Bourdaloue.............Peaches a la Bourdaloue.
415. Souffle a la Vanille..................Soufle a la Vanilla.
416. Souffle au Oatmeal.
417. Souffle a l'Americaine.
418. Poudding au Riz...... ....Rice Pudding.
419. Poudding Diplomate.
420. Plum Pudding.
421. Charlottes de Pommes............Charlotte of Apples.
422. Croute au Madere ....Toast with Madeira Sauce.
423. Pain Perdu.
424. Pommes Frittes ....Fried Apples.
425. Peches Frittes......................Fried Peaches.
426. Ananas Frit...........................Fried Pine Apple.
427. Cremes Frittes... ... .Fried Cream.
428. Pommes au Beurre ....Apples with Butter.
429. Pommes au Four.....................Baked Apples.
430. Sauce Sambayon......................Sambayon Sauce.
431. Sauce Abricot.........................Apricot Sauce.

Cold Side Dishes.

432 Riz a l'Imperatrice.................Rice a l'Imperatrice.
433. Blanc Manger.
434. Kissel a la Russe.
435. Creme au Chocolat.
436. Creme au Cafe.
437. Charlotte Russe.
438. Macedoine de Fruit.

Made in the USA
Monee, IL
06 May 2022

96017755R10092